RECOVERING JOY

Also by Kevin Griffin

One Breath at a Time: Buddhism and the Twelve Steps
(Rodale Books, 2004)

A Burning Desire: Dharma God & the Path of Recovery
(Hay House, 2010)

Buddhism & the Twelve Steps Workbook
(One Breath Books, 2014)

RECOVERING JOY

a mindful life
after addiction

Kevin Griffin

sounds true
BOULDER, COLORADO

Sounds True
Boulder, CO 80306

This work is solely for personal growth and education. It should not be treated as a substitute for professional assistance, therapeutic activities such as psychotherapy or counseling, or medical advice. In the event of physical or mental distress, please consult with appropriate health professionals. The application of protocols and information in this book is the choice of each reader, who assumes full responsibility for his or her understandings, interpretations, and results. The author and publisher assume no responsibility for the actions or choices of any reader.

Cover design by Jennifer Miles
Book design by Beth Skelley

Printed in the United States of America

Library of Congress Cataloging-in-Publication Data
Griffin, Kevin Edward, 1950–
    Recovering joy : a mindful life after addiction / Kevin Griffin.
        pages cm
    ISBN 978-1-62203-429-1
    1. Twelve-step programs—Religious aspects—Buddhism.
    2. Self-help techniques--Religious aspects—Buddhism.
    3. Happiness—Religious aspects—Buddhism.
    4. Recovering alcoholics—Psychology. I. Title.
    BQ4570.T85G744 2015
    294.3'4442—dc23
                                            2014049807

Ebook ISBN 978-1-62203-457-4

10 9 8 7 6 5 4 3 2 1

Dedicated to my daughter, Graham,
who brings me unalloyed joy.

CONTENTS

INTRODUCTION

I'm not really a happiness guy. In my teens, I found myself depressed and started to adopt a self-view as someone who was unhappy. Over the years, I wrote sad songs (which was actually kind of fun), commiserated with other depressives (which was quite comforting), and generally embraced depression and unhappiness as signs of my emotional sensitivity and realistic worldview. Nonetheless, some years ago, one of my Buddhist teachers started to talk about how we can cultivate "positive mind states." This sounded more sophisticated than merely trying to be happy, and since I'd often been in negative mind states and had a distinct distaste for them, I decided to play along.

Next thing I knew I'd been hooked into reading a book called *How We Choose to Be Happy,* just the sort of thing I would normally avoid. And, lo and behold, the thing made sense. It was practical and it resonated with my Buddhist understanding of how things work. Mainly what I got from this book was the idea that I can impact how happy I am by how I live my life. It turns out, I'm not fated to be unhappy; I can actually have an effect on my own mind states.

People in recovery from addictions—people like me—already know that our behavior affects our moods and our overall sense of well-being. If we didn't realize it before we got clean and sober, we certainly saw it afterward. Nonetheless, a recovery path like the Twelve Steps, while it's obviously about ridding ourselves of the things that make us unhappy, doesn't necessarily cultivate "positive mind states." Admitting our powerlessness, writing a moral inventory, trying to abandon character defects, and making amends are very challenging tasks. They often bring up a lot of tough feelings about ourselves. Not surprisingly, after years—and sometimes decades—of addiction, it can be easy to get stuck in judging ourselves as bad people, as people who are flawed and even undeserving of happiness.

I want to help people in recovery avoid or get out of such ways of thinking. I want to help you see that in recovery there are often already many causes for happiness that you simply need to appreciate. And I want to help you see the ways you might still be undermining yourself and to find ways to let go of these negative habits, both behaviors and ways of thinking. Maybe we can't exactly "choose" to be happy, but if we are in recovery or moving toward recovery, I think we can do a lot to make happiness—and joy and freedom—a lot more likely.

Those who know me might be chuckling right now, because I can be pretty negative myself. I sometimes say that I can turn lemonade into lemons. But I've also worked hard at creating a happy life. The elements of happiness that I'm going to describe are integral to my life. I have plenty of bad moods and difficult moments, but fundamentally I'm very contented with my life. And, in fact, remembering how good my life is, despite the moods, is one of the keys to what I define as happiness.

In this book, I want to give you ways to cultivate positive mind states and a happy life, but I don't want to be too prescriptive. In that spirit, I offer you "Reflections" that I hope will help you do a few things: first, to see how you are *already* happy; second, to understand how you get in the way of your own happiness; and third, to imagine ways you can bring more happiness and contentment into your life. I also offer "Practices," which are more active and practical ways of working with the ideas in the book, including different forms of meditation.

Reflections are opportunities to think deeply, contemplatively, and honestly about things. Much of the time in our lives we do things automatically, habitually, and reactively. We do what we've always done; we think what we've always thought or what we've been told to think; we don't engage creatively in our lives. As long as there are no big crises, we just go along thoughtlessly.

Reflection can be done by taking quiet time, whether on a solo walk in nature, a silent meditation, or just sitting back for a few moments in the middle of our day. Reflecting can happen in one of these moments, or over the course of a few days or longer, as some issue or idea keeps rolling around in our minds. What's important isn't the setting or the amount of time, but the attitude of openness and inquisitiveness. With reflecting, we try to get in touch with our deeper longings and intentions; we try to connect with the most sincere part of ourselves, with our hearts; we try to drop our defenses and fears, our judgments and assumptions. We try to understand what is really true *for us*.

Reflection can also be done with a trusted friend, sponsor, or teacher. We should always take care when we reflect with someone else that we aren't just adopting their view, or, on the other hand, reflexively rejecting their suggestions. Reflecting can be done as we listen to someone share in a Twelve Step meeting or speak in a meditation group.

Be careful, though: reflection isn't spacing out. The key to reflection is that you are *intentionally* thinking, consciously following a stream of inquiry, not just ruminating. The concept of "near enemies" can clarify this difference. A near enemy is something that *looks* similar to something else but is actually quite different. For instance, the near enemy of compassion is pity; the near enemy of equanimity is apathy. In the same way, the near enemy of reflection is rumination, a rambling semiconscious string of familiar, habitual patterns of thought. Reflection gets you somewhere new; rumination just repeats the same old fears, resentments, grievances, and fantasies.

[handwritten margin note: Contemplation / pure / understanding]

With Practices, you are usually asked to do something more specific. Many of these are meditations or at least meditative. The meditation practices in this book are based on the Buddhist teachings on mindfulness. These teachings are especially useful in looking at your own mental activity, your thoughts and feelings, your prejudices and opinions, your reactions and impulses. In tracking these patterns, we begin to free ourselves from habitual behaviors and to make more conscious choices in our lives. Mindfulness is also a key to doing the Reflections, because we need to be able to keep our minds on track and focused, not drifting off into daydreams and ruminative thought in order to reflect clearly.

This book follows what the Buddha called a "gradual path," as I build on the main elements of our lives that need to be addressed to bring happiness: integrity, relationships, work, inner life, play, health, and money. Mindfulness is addressed early on as the key tool for this work. The final chapter brings all the elements together to help you build a plan for your own happiness. At any point, you can jump to that last chapter to look at how to address any of these elements.

NOT UNHAPPY

When you hear the word *happiness,* you probably have your own sense of its meaning. Before I got sober, I thought it meant something like being in a good mood all the time or having loads of fun with no responsibilities. That's not how I define happiness now. In fact, several years ago when stuck in a long period of difficult moods, depression, and irritability, I found myself saying, "I'm depressed, but I'm not unhappy." What did that mean?

What I was saying was that nothing was wrong with my life. I was healthy, had a loving family that I adored, and found great satisfaction in my work. I understood by that time that troubling moods seemed to be a persistent, if intermittent, part of my life, but that they didn't impinge on the essential value and meaning of my life or the satisfaction I derived from it. I think it has partly been this attitude toward moods that has allowed me to be less controlled by them.

So, obviously, I'm saying that happiness isn't just a mood. That doesn't mean we can be happy without ever being in a good mood. Certainly having access to joyful and uplifting feelings on a fairly regular basis is part of what I'd call happiness. But happiness is more than that. I think it includes and depends upon the following elements, which are also the main chapters of this book:

- Integration of values and behavior; that is, we live up to our own moral and ethical standards without "shadow" behaviors. We're not hiding any part of our lives from those close to us.

- Satisfying interpersonal relationships, be they with a partner, friends, family, or coworkers; our spiritual community; and our teachers, sponsors, and other healers.

- Satisfying work that both challenges us and allows us to use our intelligence and creativity to their fullest extent.

- A rich inner life that includes a sense of connection to something greater than ourselves, be that a religious or spiritual connection, or simply a sense of connection with the human race, other beings, or just nature. This may include meditation or a creative practice.

- An element of fun in our lives. As adults, many of us neglect this vital element of happiness.

- A healthy relationship to money and basic financial security, and good self-care of our bodies, including diet and healing.

- A sense of purpose and our own value. This may express itself through our work and how we see ourselves contributing to the world, or it may express itself in our relationships—the way we help and care for others.

all eudaimonia {

For addicts in recovery, this list in some sense provides a parallel process to the Twelve Steps. The Steps require us to face our moral and ethical lapses, and they also show us how living with integrity is so much more easeful than otherwise; certainly most of us have had to do a lot of work repairing interpersonal relationships; many of us have to spend years getting our work lives sorted out and straightening out our finances; as addicts, we often neglect our bodies, and need to learn how to care for them in recovery; spiritual connection is an essential part of the groundwork of recovery in the Twelve Steps; and learning how to have fun and play without intoxicants is one of the first challenges of recovery.

The Buddha defines happiness in many different ways. First, he acknowledges that there is a certain pleasure to be found in the sense life: taste, touch, smell, sight, and sound. In our culture, this is usually depicted as the beginning and end of the source of happiness, but the Buddha characterizes sense pleasure as "coarse," lacking subtlety, and ultimately unsatisfying, *dukkha* (a word often translated as "suffering," but which has no exact English equivalent). While it's true that sense pleasures are all impermanent, I don't think lay people have to be so quick to write them off. Most of us need a certain amount of this comfort to maintain positive mind states. These pleasures can come from all the senses: seeing a beautiful sunset or stunning painting; getting carried away listening to a singer who moves us deeply; letting go into the bliss of orgasm; or soaking in a flood of endorphins at the end of a workout. It can come from tasting a good cup of coffee or savoring a piece of chocolate. The Buddha said there was "gratification, danger, and escape" with these pleasures: the gratification is the actual pleasure; the danger is that we get attached to that pleasure, because no matter what, it can't last, so if we're attached we'll always end up disappointed; the escape is letting go of that attachment. The point is, enjoy sense pleasures, but don't see them as the ultimate source of your happiness or freedom. Unfortunately, as addicts, that's exactly how we did see them, trying to find and hold onto happiness in a bottle, a pill, a line of powder, or a puff of smoke.

More pleasurable than sense experience, according to the Buddha, is the joy of calm, abiding, meditative peace. Because this state is one where there's no sense of lack, and thus no craving for things to be different from how they are, the Buddha sees this as a greater form of happiness than more excited states where craving is present. I think

7

that for many of us, it was the promise of such peace that drew us to meditation in the first place. For me, calm abiding continues to be a great source of happiness and gratification. But don't be fooled: Cultivating rich meditative states requires real dedication. In order to access and maintain them, most people need to go on regular silent retreats. It's much easier to pop a pill or roll a joint than it is to develop calm abiding, so naturally a lot more people take the easy route. Again, for addicts, we know the futility of the quick approach to finding happiness, and that's one of the reasons we are willing to do challenging Twelve Step work. It's this same hard-won wisdom that brings people to Buddhist recovery work, the recognition that the promise of happiness in money, sex, fame, or success is empty.

In the Buddha's hierarchy of happiness, insight tops even peaceful meditation for bringing happiness, because it frees us from clinging. The ultimate insight is the ultimate letting-go: nirvana, the ultimate happiness. And while this ultimate insight may have eluded me, I've certainly had many moments of nonultimate insight, revealing truths about my own psychology and behavior, all the places where I get stuck; my practice has also opened me to the universal truths of suffering, impermanence, and corelessness that the Buddha said underlie all experience. A great sense of ease comes with these insights, as we see the truth clearly and are able, at least for a moment, to step out of our personal drama into a broad view of reality. Here the suffering of the headlines and the confusion of our inner lives are both seen as an expression of the same fundamental patterns of life, and, even though nothing may change on the outside, with these insights our whole perspective can shift, like watching a movie and suddenly remembering that it's all just a projection of pictures and sound, actors reciting a script, lighting and costumes and sets.

In some fundamental way, it's balancing this ultimate view with the practical realities of life that I see as the Buddhist path to wisdom and happiness. I have to take care of the practical world and commit fully to living skillfully, while at the same time holding a broad, impersonal view so that this world of pleasure and pain doesn't hypnotize me with craving or swamp me with despair.

In talking about these stages or levels of happiness, the Buddha gives instruction for each level. Like my own list, he lays down morality as a fundamental necessity for building a happy and beneficial life; whether for monastics or laypeople, he tells us that maintaining loving, supportive, and responsible relationships and a strong community is central to our spiritual development; he describes skillful forms of livelihood and the importance of generosity and service; and of course he teaches a wide range of contemplative and meditative practices to cultivate skillful mind states and openheartedness.

What the Buddha is pointing to, just like the Twelve Steps and other recovery programs, is that our happiness isn't just dependent on our life circumstances or emotional tendencies. While these certainly have a part, it is our own choices and actions that can swing the pendulum toward happiness. Happiness may not be our birthright, but for most of us, it's within reach if we are willing to do the work.

REFLECTION   **What Is Happiness?**

Before you do this exercise, ask yourself what you would add to the list of elements of happiness below. Then include any additional aspects in this reflection.

Take some time to review the list of elements of happiness:

- Integrity
- Healthy relationships
- Gratifying work
- Spiritual practice
- Fun
- Healthy relationship to body and to money
- Other

Notice where you already have these things in your life and where you don't. Where you don't have these things, consider actions you can take to achieve them. Make the commitment today to begin to bring these things into your life. Remember, "One day at a time." Happiness doesn't come overnight. Begin to lay the foundation today, and try to maintain the long view. ▪

REFLECTION   **What Is My Happiness?**

Begin by reflecting on how you define happiness. I've found that many people don't even like the term *happy*, or feel that it's not a realistic goal. I, too, had to find my own way of understanding what it meant to be happy. Maybe you're more comfortable with a different word: *joy* or *contentment* or *well-being*. See what works for you. I believe we all want some version of happiness or okayness, some sense of enjoying or feeling good about our lives and ourselves.

Now take some time to ask yourself what you really want from your life. This isn't about money or fame or even, really, about worldly success of any kind. It's more about how we live.

Think back over the moments in your life that brought you great joy; consider periods of time when you felt most contented or engaged in your life; and remember those times when you were *unhappy*, so that you can gain some perspective over causes and conditions for your own happiness. Are you doing the things that make you happy? Could you restart some past activity that brought you happiness?

Of course, you may not be able to go back to specific activities you used to do. For instance, you might love kids but be past the child-bearing age, so perhaps you could volunteer at a preschool or teach kindergarten. Maybe your knees won't let you run anymore, so you could take up bicycle riding or hiking. Bringing this kind of joy into our lives may take a certain amount of creativity, but that too can be some of the pleasure of the process, just reflecting on what makes us happy. ▪

Taking Joy

No matter how together our lives are, how good they look, how much stuff or success or fame we have, if we can't take joy in it, we won't be happy. Taking joy is the realm of mindfulness, the Buddhist practice that underlies all the ideas in this book. Mindfulness is fundamentally about being present for our life, for each moment in a wholehearted, nonreactive, inquisitive, and intuitive way. While mindfulness is an inherent human capacity that we all have, it's something most of us have never developed and need guidance and practice to establish. Mindfulness training is done formally in meditation, and it can be done informally in all activities, like walking, talking, eating, or exercising. Anything we do, we can do mindfully, and mindfulness enhances the experience of any activity.

With mindfulness, we actually experience the joy in our lives. We taste our food more fully; we feel our emotions more clearly; we see the beauty around us and are touched by sorrow, joy, and pleasure. Mindfulness enriches every moment.

When we take joy, we remind ourselves to fully experience something. I often find it amusing when I'm at some beautiful natural site and people pull out their cameras. Instead of actually experiencing the beauty, they are trying to capture it and take it home. How silly. As if looking at a picture of the Grand Canyon or the Golden Gate could be more satisfying than actually being there. And yet, if we don't learn how to be fully present, to be mindful, this is often the best we can do. When we are numbed by the constant inflow of sense experiences that our culture provides, it can become hard to feel anything more than superficially.

For me, it was only after I'd gone on a Buddhist meditation retreat in California that I started to discover this kind of engagement. Returning to my hometown in Pennsylvania for Christmas, I was shocked to see how beautiful it was. I'd never noticed the loveliness of the brick sidewalks, the Victorian mansions, the tree-lined streets, and the eighteenth-century church. I realized that I'd sleepwalked through my life until then, caught up in my own thoughts and feelings, taking my surroundings for granted. I finally began to take joy in the world around me.

In my role as a spiritual teacher, I've been fortunate to have the opportunity to perform a few marriages. Each time I do, I try to emphasize to the couple the importance of being present and taking joy in the moments of the ceremony. Especially with experiences like getting married, with all the excitement, stress, and trappings, it's easy to get lost and forget to pay attention. These are precious moments that only come once (hopefully), and we must remember to fully take in their joy. As a musician, I used to play at weddings from time to time, and seeing the bride or groom getting drunk was particularly tragic to me for this very reason.

Here's another, much simpler example of taking joy: when I eat a piece of high-quality chocolate, I stop and savor it, smelling the chocolate, inhaling the flavor, rolling my tongue over the smooth texture, chewing slowly, and taking in the whole pleasurable experience. *Ahh!*

PRACTICE   One Pleasant Thing (OPT)

"Sacred Pause"
"affirmation,
optimism,
options"

Sometimes all it takes to make a shift in mood is to notice something you can enjoy right now. I call this practice "One Pleasant Thing," or OPT. OPT can be a thought or memory, a mood or uplifting emotion. OPT can be a pleasant sensation in the body, the feel of the breeze on your face, the sound of children playing, or the light as it comes through the leaves of a tree. I find that stepping outside helps me to find OPT. When we intentionally look for something pleasant, we can usually find it.

We have to be careful with OPT that we aren't trying, in that addictive way, to create a constant stream of pleasant experiences. Everything can't always be pleasant. When things are difficult, they are difficult—no getting around it. OPT is most useful for more-neutral states or moments of boredom. In those moments, sometimes all we need is a slight shift of perspective to bring an uplift to our day.

I like that OPT reminds us to find something positive in this moment, like an *optimist,* and that it shows us that we have *options* as to what we focus on. ■

✴ PRACTICE **Smile Like a Buddha** (aka "Inner Smile")

A good way to trigger OPT is to smile. We see that in statues of the Buddha he often has a slight, wry smile. What is he thinking? The way we answer that question might tell us some interesting things about ourselves.

I learned to bring Buddha's smile to my face in meditation and was amazed by how well it worked. It would actually lift my mood to smile; it also turned out to support the development of concentration. Soon I learned to adopt the smile in my daily life—not to force a smile, but, again, as with any OPT, when I'm in a neutral or inattentive state. From that place, the smile can have a very effective mood-lifting effect.

As a natural pessimist and cynic, I admit that if people say, "Come on, smile!" I just get more irritated. So if I hadn't learned this practice in a formal meditation, I probably would never have done it. The Vietnamese Zen Master Thich Nhat Hanh teaches a meditation practice called "Present Moment Wonderful Moment" where I first learned this practice. You can find it in his book of the same name or in my book *A Burning Desire*.

> When you step outside in the morning,
> look at the world and smile.
>
> When you see a baby, smile.
>
> When you hear music you love, smile.
>
> When you see people you love, smile.
>
> Smile like a Buddha. ∎

Varieties of Mindfulness

Mindfulness has become something of a blanket term to refer to any activity done with clarity and awareness, whether it's sitting meditation, mindful movement, mindful eating, or anything else. In exploring these different forms, it makes sense to start with formal mindfulness meditation, which will help you to understand what mindfulness is and to have a deeper experience of mindfulness. This understanding will then inform other practices of mindfulness.

We can explore mindfulness meditation quite deeply, given the time and circumstances to do so. It opens us to the life of the mind and body in ways unparalleled in ordinary human experience. Many books have been written on the topic, and some people spend years working with and developing an understanding of this practice.

On the other hand, in its essence mindfulness can be fairly easily described: be here now. This famous phrase, coined more than forty years ago by the psychologist cum guru Richard Alpert/Ram Dass, remains the perfect pith of the practice—so simple and yet so challenging to achieve. Our attempts to follow this instruction lead us to many of the insights that Buddhism points to: our minds are very busy, even out of control; our bodies are restless, ever searching for comfort; "now" is not a stable thing because everything keeps changing; and our reactivity and desire for things to be different from the way they are cause us ongoing stress and discomfort. Working with these challenging experiences is what makes mindfulness meditation difficult, but also what pushes us deeper into the practice.

There are plenty of resources available today for learning mindfulness, including my own Sounds True recordings, so I won't elaborate too much on the mechanics of the meditation practice. I also think that trying to learn to meditate from reading words on a page is not the most effective method. Best is to have a live teacher, and second best is a recording. You'll find information on meditation centers and online tools in the Other Recommended Resources section at the back of the book. Nonetheless, let me just outline the basics of getting started with mindfulness meditation.

PRACTICE **Mindfulness Meditation**

Find a quiet place where you can sit undisturbed. Sit in a posture that is upright and reasonably comfortable. Close your eyes, or if you don't like to close your eyes or if you are sleepy, just lower your gaze. Try to let your body relax, and as you do so, feel yourself settling. Feel your body breathing. Let your attention focus on one point of sensation in your breathing, either the tip of the nose, where the air comes in and out, or in the belly, as it rises and falls. If you're following the breath at the nose, feel the sensation of air touching the nostrils as it comes in and out. If you're following the breath at the belly, feel the movement as the ribs expand and the belly rhythmically moves.

When you notice that your attention has wandered from the breath, acknowledge that and bring your attention back to the breath. Try not to judge or criticize yourself for the thoughts you are having, because that just becomes another thought that distracts you.

Each time you find yourself lost and return to the sensations of breath, relax into your body, settle back, and start again.

FIVE HINDRANCES

In the classical Buddhist teachings on mindfulness meditation, the Five Hindrances are said to obstruct the development of calm, concentration, and insight. The challenges they describe remain relevant to our practice today:

- Desire: the energy of craving; plans, fantasies, self-centered wishes

- Aversion: the energy of resistance; judging and resenting; impatience and irritability; negativity and ill will

- Sloth and Torpor: sleepiness in the body; dullness in the mind; dreaminess, disinterest, apathy

- Restlessness and Worry: agitation in the body; anxiety in the mind; obsessive thinking and fear

- Doubt: skepticism of the teacher or the teaching; questioning your own capacity to meditate, recover, or do a spiritual practice

That's it. Certainly there's much more that can be said about this form of meditation, but most of it has to do with dealing with the so-called distractions that arise. The reason they are "so-called" is that with mindfulness, we don't so much try to separate ourselves from the world of thoughts, feelings, and perceptions as simply watch it all come and go. Learning to do this takes lots of practice, so patience and commitment are essential aspects of the practice.

Other mindfulness practices spin out from this one, using the same essential premise to be present, to notice our reactions and digressions from that presence, and to return again to the activity at hand. So, with mindful movement, we focus on the body, the sensations of movement and energies within. When the attention wanders, we bring it back to those sensations. With mindful eating, we follow the experience of craving and hunger, and then pay attention to taste, smell, texture, and pleasure in eating, trying to stay connected enough with our bodies that we eat only what we need, not mindlessly gobbling up what we don't.

There are obvious connections, then, to psychotherapy, as mindfulness helps us to see which habitual thoughts keep arising and to explore the roots and branches of those thoughts. When combined with traditional cognitive therapy, this approach has shown great results in dealing with depressive moods.

As someone who is committed to and immersed in Buddhist teachings, I don't see mindfulness as the cure-all it is sometimes characterized as. As just one aspect of the Eightfold Path, the Buddha's teaching on how to live and find freedom, mindfulness is much more useful when developed as an integral part of that system of morality, meditation, and wisdom. If we aren't living with integrity, mindfulness will be of peripheral benefit; if we want mindfulness only as a palliative, we'll lose a great deal of the value; and if we aren't able to bring a broad view of our experience, putting it in the greater context of life and the human experience, we will miss the true meaning of this work. Mindfulness is the starting point and essential tool for putting this all together, but it doesn't stand alone. ∎

WALK THE TALK

integrating values and behavior

As addicts, one of the greatest conflicts we face when lost in our addiction is knowing that we aren't living up to our own values and beliefs. We *want* to be good people, to do the right thing, but we just can't. This is the power of addiction: to seemingly force us to act against our own best intentions. Nobody wants to be an addict, but we wind up there anyway. Getting clean and sober, or getting free of whatever our addictive behavior was, is the first big step in resolving this conflict.

But the Twelve Steps, or any recovery path, are about much more than just giving up a particular behavior. There are many elements of recovery, but the first one is bringing our behavior into alignment with our values. From a Twelve Step perspective, this includes the entire inventory and amends process.

Giving Up — *"Lent, 2020"*

I woke up happy on June 7, 1985, the first time I'd felt good first thing in the morning in at least six months. You wouldn't think I'd have been in a very positive state of mind after getting fired from a gig the night before and coming home to sleep off the booze and pot.

But somewhere between the last beer and first light, I had given up. I'd given up drinking, I'd given up pot, I'd given up cocaine.

Like any big letting-go, this one had been a long time coming. I'd been trying to control my drinking and using for many, many years, and even as my addictions had persisted I'd pursued spiritual answers to my life's problems.

That morning, the battle between my addiction and my spiritual longing resolved itself in the deep and profound letting-go of surrender. And in that surrender was great joy, the joy the Buddha explains is the result of letting go of craving and clinging.

It's all right there in the Four Noble Truths, the starting point of all Buddhist teachings and insights: clinging causes suffering; letting go brings freedom. But for an addict, this concept can seem beyond comprehension. When we're driven by the compulsion to drink and use, to eat or gamble, to control others or to be loved by them, the answer seems to be just the opposite—we need to try harder, strive more fiercely, grasp tighter. We *have* to have *it,* whatever it is, or we'll suffer.

So, there I was in my cottage in Venice Beach, California, on a beautiful June morning, and I was smiling. Broke, unemployed, and happy. Once again proving the Buddha's point that happiness doesn't come from stuff or from success or from pleasant experiences, but from our attitude, our relationship to what is. The specific cause of my happiness that morning was the feeling of relief that I didn't have to try to control my drinking and using anymore. I hadn't realized how much of a burden that effort had been, day after day, year after year, going back to my teens (I was 35 at the time). Although I hadn't been able to imagine living without booze and pot, now it was like a curtain being lifted, and I saw clearly that there was nothing to fear and everything to gain, that getting loaded had stopped being fun a long time ago, and that the fear of stopping and the compulsion to keep using were the only things left that had kept me going in my addictions. Finally having the courage—or whatever it was—to let go allowed me to enter into this moment of joy and freedom.

When people talk at Twelve Step meetings about their early recovery, it's often about the struggles to stay clean, the problems they faced, and the devastating "wreckage of the past" they had to acknowledge. All of this is real, but equally real is the great relief of letting go.

When looking for joy in recovery, the first place we find it is in this relief. That's why many people, when they discover the joy of dropping their addiction, start to give up other unhealthy habits, like smoking or eating lots of junk food. We may find ourselves taking a whole new approach to our lives, looking for things to give up. In the Buddhist tradition, this is called "renunciation," and although in our culture that term seems to have negative connotations of deprivation and asceticism, from the standpoint of

THE FOUR NOBLE TRUTHS

honor / respect

1. The Truth of Suffering: life is full of challenges and inevitable loss.

2. The Truth of the Cause of Suffering: psychological suffering comes from the persistent craving for things to be different from how they are.

3. The Truth of the End of Suffering: when we can let go of craving and accept things as they are, this suffering can end, at least in that moment of acceptance.

   Ecstasy: "the temporary alleviation of misery."

4. The Truth of the Way to the End of Suffering: the Buddha's Eightfold Path of integrity, mind training, and wisdom.

   "pure understanding"

the Second Noble Truth, it's the clearest way to happiness. That's why the monastic life is built around simplicity—around letting go of many of the supposed comforts of life. What the monastics know, and what people in recovery have insight into, is the truth that happiness doesn't come from the things we have, but from the abandoning of the things we cling to, the things that hold us down and capture our minds.

REFLECTION **Taking Joy in Giving Up**

This is a simple reflection: think, write, and talk about the early moments of gratification in your recovery. If it's been a while, sit down or take a walk and review what those early moments and days were like. Sure, there were probably some tough times, but for most of us, there was also real relief.

Once you've recalled that time, you might want to share this at a meeting or with a friend.

Why stay in recovery if it doesn't make you happy? Stay connected to that simple joy of letting go. ▪

"It feels so good to be SOBER today. I'm glad to be SOBER now." SINCERITY.

REFLECTION   **The Joy of Letting Go**

The next time you meditate (which I hope is today or tomorrow), pay special attention to the moment of letting go. Notice how you feel when you catch a thought, let it go, and come back to the breath. Take pleasure in that moment, and realize that what you are seeing is the truth of the Second and Third Noble Truths: that what causes suffering is clinging, and what frees us from suffering is letting go.

Notice the tension in the body that releases as you return to the breath. Notice the emotional release that happens. And notice that nothing is lost, that whatever the thought was, it really wasn't so important that you couldn't drop it.

When a thought is so stubborn that you can't drop it, notice the persistence of suffering, of tension in the body, of anxiety in the mind. When you do this, you are having the same insight—that clinging causes suffering. Sometimes we simply can't let go because we are so habituated to our fears, resentments, and grief. Please don't add to your suffering by judging yourself for this. It's perfectly natural and happens to all of us. Meditation isn't about perfection, but if we keep seeing how suffering arises through clinging, we'll grow more and more willing to let go, even of those things that used to obsess us. ▪

Return to Innocence — *silence*

Once we've let go of our substance abuse or habitual behavior, many of us start to see other imbalances in our lives. Part of addiction is often a cavalier attitude toward morality in general. When we are loaded, we tend to act out sexually; we can be violent and abusive; we might steal or just avail ourselves of other people's property, like their drugs.

When we let ourselves be driven by the greed of addiction, that drive bleeds into everything else in our lives. We live in a culture that glorifies wealth, sex, and pleasure, so it's no wonder people fall into habits of selfishness and greed.

I grew up a good little Catholic boy who wanted to avoid "sin." As a teenager, I turned away from those values just at the time that I turned toward alcohol and drugs. Soon enough, the question "What is right and wrong?" morphed into "What do I want and how can I get it?"

As I transitioned into adulthood, my childhood pleasures, like sports, school, and family, lost their appeal. Now I wanted adult pleasures: drinking, drugging, smoking, and sex. I'm not unique in this. I recently heard someone in a meeting talk about becoming a habitual drinker at the age of ten; it struck me how childhood is often a rush to grow up, not realizing what we are losing.

Noah Levine tells such a story in his gripping spiritual memoir *Dharma Punx*. His harrowing childhood included the urge to commit suicide before he'd reached third grade. By his late teens, addicted to drugs, violence, and a life driven by hatred, he wound up in juvenile hall. There he began the remarkable turnaround that resulted in his becoming a leading spiritual teacher and an inspiration to a whole generation of people disillusioned with our culture. Today, covered in tattoos and clad in the uniform of a rebellious punk rocker, Noah speaks beautifully about forgiveness, lovingkindness, and recovery. As a father of two, and with "Will you marry me?" tattooed on his neck, he exemplifies the sweetness that can come with a dedication to recovery.

This is why I sometimes call recovery "a return to innocence"—although for some, like Noah, there never was much innocence to begin with. I thought growing up and being able to drink, take drugs, and have sex was what life was about. But, at least for this addict, those behaviors were never the answer. I had everything I needed as a child, but I didn't know it. I threw it all away when I grew up, and it took a long time to get it all back.

When I was in high school, everything gradually fell apart. I started experiencing depression and lost interest in school. I started drinking and drugging, and the only joy I had left was playing music. I decided I would become a professional musician because it seemed like the only thing that I enjoyed anymore. At fourteen, I joined my first rock 'n' roll band and started playing at high school dances and college frat parties. It seemed pretty glamorous. In fact, I joined that band, The Squires, just months after seeing The Beatles on *The Ed Sullivan Show,* so I was joining a huge cultural movement. Of course, playing music is a wonderful way to experience joy, and there's nothing wrong with it. But for me, it became my identity and my sole source of meaning and happiness. Soon my grades began to slip. In tenth grade, I got mononucleosis, missed a month of school, and flunked. I never made it through another year of high school, dropping out each of the next three years.

By then, I'd convinced myself that I hated school and that as a future rock star, I had no need for it. It would take twenty years for me to find my way back. Then, at three years sober, I enrolled in community college. I started with basics like English composition, algebra, and geography. Although I'd always had an affinity for English, math and science had held no interest for me—until then. I was amazed to find myself completely engaged in these topics, which as a teenager had seemed so dry and pointless. I had to think back to an even earlier time, preteen, when everything actually interested me. I was experiencing my return to innocence. I was experiencing the joy of learning. Once again, I saw how both my addiction to drugs and alcohol and the limiting ideas about myself that seemed to accompany that had drained all the joy from my life, had narrowed my world down to my guitar, my beer and pot, the bars I played, and the women I sought.

I don't know if this idea of a return to innocence will resonate for a lot of people. For me, it feels like simplifying, dropping the complications of life. It's interesting that many of the activities that are legally only allowed for adults—drinking, smoking, gambling, and "adult entertainment"—are all potentially addictive. I suppose it makes sense that we want to protect young people from the dangers associated with these

activities, but it's also somewhat sad that once we come of age, these can *wu-wei, Zazen*
become our main ways of finding pleasure in our lives.

In Buddhist meditation, our practice is very simple: pay attention to the breath, let thoughts fade away (hopefully), and just be. There's certainly no entertainment, adult or otherwise, in this practice. Further, in those moments of real stillness or emptiness that occasionally occur through these efforts, we can wonder why the Buddha is encouraging us to develop this emptiness. Nothing seems to be going on; we're not figuring anything out or seemingly accomplishing anything. What's the point?

"Doing Nothing"

Perhaps one of the points, at least, is to rest in this innocence, the uncreated, the nondoing state. At first this state might seem useless or meaningless, but if we bring the same attention to the experience of what Ayya Khema, the remarkable German Buddhist nun, called "Being Nobody, Going Nowhere," we experience the great relief, the deep peace and pleasure that nondoing brings. This purity, this emptiness, is what Mahayana Buddhists call "Buddha Nature" and Tibetans call "Basic Goodness." These terms fundamentally express the Buddhist principle that when we take away all the negative qualities of mind—craving, aversion, and delusion—what's left is a luminous, pure state of being, a state that lacks nothing and needs abandon nothing. I call this state innocence. *"I call it silence." "no-form" "magnanimity" "equanimity" · integrity*

Who I Want to Be

When I got sober, I thought I was pretty special. I thought that the fact that I'd already been practicing meditation for years, and had even gone on some long retreats and hung around with Buddhist teachers, made me different from the rest of the people I was encountering in Twelve Step meetings. I thought that, unlike them, I'd always been on a spiritual journey, but that they were just discovering spirituality. It was only when I started to teach about integrating Twelve Step work with Buddhism that I discovered how limited and egotistical a view this was.

What I find today is that many people who come to recovery programs have been quite serious, or at least semiserious, about their spiritual practice already. Many have tried meditation, at least off and on, for years, others have strong religious or spiritual beliefs, and most have pretty clear moral values that they, unfortunately, haven't been able to live up to. Some, like me, have gotten caught at some point in cultlike, delusional, or magical belief systems. The point is, though, that whether they were alcoholics, drug addicts, food addicts, sex addicts, gambling addicts, codependents, or adult children of alcoholics, their "disease" didn't define them. It didn't mean that they were bad or fundamentally immoral or even amoral people; it simply meant that the power of their addiction was stronger than the power of their commitment to their values.

This is why we talk about being "powerless" over our addiction. Drugs and alcohol and all the other addictive behaviors get a grip on our minds and hearts and pull us away from who we really want to be.

If what we are seeking is happiness or joy in recovery, we will never find it until we start to live in harmony with our values. We could say that, from a Twelve Step perspective, besides being about the inventory and amends process, this is also about "turning it over," Step Three. This means we are not going to allow our cravings and resentments to control our behavior; we are instead going to bring our actions into harmony with our values and beliefs. I don't know if this sounds easy, but it isn't. Craving and resentment, or greed and hatred, are the energies that pretty much run the world—war, exploitation, luxury, and lust, these are what run economics and politics; they are pretty much what defines human history. To think we can just "make a decision" to stop being driven by these energies is either naïve or arrogant.

This is why there is a program and a practice, why there are Steps and meditations, retreats and classes, sponsors and teachers, and all our supportive friends. But even with all that, if living in harmony with our values didn't bring joy, what would be the point? That joy is what I want you to know, to realize, and to experience.

Maybe waking up clearheaded, able to remember falling asleep the night before, doesn't strike you as worth much, but I remember realizing in my third year of recovery that that's exactly how I'd been living since giving up drinking, and I had a moment of appreciation. Maybe driving somewhere at night with no fear of being pulled over for a DUI doesn't give you a thrill, but next time you're doing that, just remember the stress and ugliness of driving drunk or stoned. Maybe telling your boss *exactly* how you screwed up doesn't hold much allure, but the next time you have that opportunity, notice the relief of not having to lie or cover up, the freedom from shame when we can simply be human, imperfect. Maybe not feeling compelled to sleep with, or at least try to sleep with, every attractive person you meet doesn't seem like a source of joy, but recollect closing time at the bar when that craving was so painful that you were willing to go to bed with a stranger who wasn't even very appealing to you. It's these recollections, these moments of letting go, that bring the soft, subtle joy of recovery, the contentment of knowing your life makes sense, that there aren't shadows and shame, lies and crimes that must be hidden from others and suppressed in your own mind.

Integrating values and behavior can take many forms. A favorite story that exemplifies the simplicity of this change is one I heard at a Twelve Step meeting. "My program," said one of the participants, "is to return my shopping cart after I put the groceries in my car." Somehow this simple, even trivial commitment seemed to me to epitomize what recovery is about. Not the big moments or accomplishments, not even the big amends or inventory or "spiritual awakenings." Just being a good citizen, someone who cares enough not to leave his shopping cart out in the middle of the parking lot, making it someone else's problem. Addicts seem to be all about leaving things to be someone else's problem. In recovery, we finally begin to take responsibility for our actions. And there is real joy in that, in knowing we are doing the right thing.

REFLECTION **Who I Want to Be**

Take some time to consider whether you are living with integrity and honesty. If not, why not? What are the drives that pull you toward unwholesome behavior? Is it possible you would be happier if you made more of a commitment to follow your deeper intentions? ■

The Truth, the Whole Truth, and Nothing but the Truth

When I first showed up at a Twelve Step meeting, I was shocked by the level of honesty. It wasn't so much the secrets or even the horrifying stories of alcoholic depravity that shocked me, but just the willingness of people to speak openly about how crappy they felt. On top of that, there was a willingness to admit failings and failures that I couldn't imagine having. And, indeed, it would take me more than a year of hanging out in the back of the room before I finally took my seat in front and opened up.

Speaking the truth is vital to recovery, as lies and secrets are so tied into our addiction. The Buddha, too, emphasized speaking the truth. Right Speech is both an element of the Eightfold Path and one of the Five Precepts. While many people think that silent meditation is the key to Buddhist practice, the Buddha's focus on skillful and honest speech tells another story.

There are several aspects of truth telling involved in recovery and happiness. The first is telling ourselves the truth. Denial is a kind of lying to ourselves, an unwillingness to admit to ourselves that we have a problem.

THE EIGHTFOLD PATH

1. Right View: seeing reality wisely, free from denial

2. Right Intention: trying to follow the wisdom we develop with Right View

3. Right Speech: speaking the truth kindly and in a timely manner

4. Right Action: following the Five Precepts

5. Right Livelihood: work that is nonharming and serves society and ourselves

6. Right Effort: letting go of harmful mind states and cultivating skillful ones

7. Right Mindfulness: wise attention to body and mind

8. Right Concentration: focus, calm, and stillness

When confronted by others with my failings before I got sober, I reacted with anger. This is how I protected myself. I can still be defensive, though that stance isn't nearly so impermeable as it was those decades ago.

Why do I get angry? Anger is a reaction to a threat, and criticism is a threat to the ego. If I am dependent upon or attached to a view that I must be beyond reproach to be okay, then any whiff of criticism is a threat. This is one of the reasons why recovery must start with admitting we have a problem. The walls built around the ego must be dismantled if we are going to

THE FIVE PRECEPTS OF NONHARMING

1. I take the training precept to refrain from killing any living being.

2. I take the training precept to refrain from taking that which is not given.

3. I take the training precept to refrain from sexual misconduct.

4. I take the training precept to refrain from false or harmful speech.

5. I take the training precept to refrain from the use of intoxicants.

change. We have to be willing to see ourselves truthfully, the good and the bad, before we can find peace in the world.

The next form of truth is speaking the truth to others. To addicts, truth is somewhat fungible, since our main goal is to stay loaded and get what we want. When we are working a program, we start to take responsibility for our actions, and so speaking the truth becomes part of that commitment.

In trying to speak the truth, we need to address the question of what we really know versus what is just an opinion or a conditioned viewpoint. The Buddha talks about the importance of "not holding to fixed views," and that as long as we are attached to our opinions we can't be free. This is why mindfulness of our thoughts and words is so important. When we start to examine our thoughts, we begin to separate the conditioned ideas from what is really true.

In speaking the truth, we need to also hold the Buddha's other instructions on Right Speech in mind, particularly not to harm others with speech. When I was young, I liked to use the truth as a weapon. I justified this by saying that I just wanted to be completely honest. Of course, there's a reason why this is called "brutal" honesty. If there's no good reason to tell someone such a "truth," then we are wise to remain silent.

When speaking of truth from a Buddhist perspective, we can talk about relative truth and absolute truth. Most of the things we talk about are in the realm of the relative, but it's important to keep absolute truth in mind as well, to reflect on teachings like the Three Characteristics, the three core insights of Buddhism. They point out that everything in life is impermanent, ultimately unsatisfying, and without core identity. (More about the Three Characteristics can be found in chapter 5.) The Dharma, the absolute truth, gives us the broadest perspective on our lives and on reality. It allows us to step back from the melee of everyday life and see things in this more objective, impersonal way, which can be very freeing when we find ourselves caught up in the story of our lives.

The spiritual path is sometimes called a search for truth. If we are going to find happiness and peace in our lives, this search demands "rigorous honesty," with ourselves and others, as well as an adherence to these larger truths.

PRACTICE **Mindful Speech**

Developing the skills of mindful speech is a long-term process. We need to understand the elements of Right Speech—speaking the truth, at the right time, and only if useful and kind—and then we need to be present moment-by-moment in interactions to avoid falling into habitual ways of speaking. This points to the fact that speech starts inside as thoughts, which means we need to watch our thoughts before speaking and during conversations. Mindful speech includes mindful listening, being able to close our mouths and open our minds. Mindful speech requires sensitivity, compassion, and an intention to use speech for good purposes.

Besides watching our minds before and during speech, we need to take our time, trying not to speak reactively or impulsively, but with clear intention.

All of this may seem beyond our capacity, and many times, it probably is. But if we can apply these principles sometimes and use them as a reference point all the time, we will gradually become more accustomed and skillful at speaking and listening with wise attention. ▪

It's All About Karma

Actions bring results. That's the Law of Karma, one of Buddhism's central teachings. There's no destiny or fate involved in this law—simply action and the motivation behind the action. Drink or use or gamble or binge time after time and a habit develops; day after day and an addiction develops; year after year and a compulsion takes over. Whenever we do something or think something or feel something over and over, the tendency to do, think, or feel that thing gets stronger and stronger—this is the simple process of developing an addiction. Whenever we *don't* do or think or feel something over and over, or whenever we let go of a behavior, thought pattern, or emotional habit, the weaker the tendency to act, think, or feel in that way becomes. This is the simple process of recovery. If we are going to not just get into recovery, but find happiness there, we are going to have to recognize the truth of the Law of Karma and work in harmony with it. And *work* is the operative word here.

There's no magic to finding happiness or recovery. It's about showing up. If you want it, you've got to do it. The Twelve Steps are called "a program of action." The Buddha's Eightfold Path is also one of action. In fact, the Buddha said that if it weren't possible for us to find freedom through our own actions, he wouldn't even teach his dharma. He said that it was up to each of us to do this work for ourselves, that he couldn't do it for us. There's no magic out there that can fix you; there's no prayer that will win you the lottery; there's no super-being that will solve all your problems. In fact, if there's any "Higher Power," it is this Law of Karma itself. It is "turning our will and our lives" over to this that gives us real power and relief. This means we need to understand how karma works and then make the effort to live in harmony with it. The entire Eightfold Path, not to mention the Twelve Steps, is about activating positive karma through our actions. As Buddhadasa Bhikkhu says, change and growth happen when we "beseech the Law of Karma through our actions, not merely with words."

Before having us take action, the Eightfold Path starts with Right View and Right Intention. Right View is seeing the truth, how actions bring results, how clinging causes suffering, how things are constantly changing, and how attaching to a view of self entraps us. With Right View, we come out of denial and see how we need to refocus our lives, so taking Step One in recovery is an expression of Right View.

Once we see how things work through this initial insight, we develop Right Intention, setting the goal of living in harmony with the truth we have seen in Right View. Right Intention is just that: a *wish* to do the right thing, which implies that we won't always succeed, but that when we do fall off the path (or the wagon), we will return to these guiding principles. The Buddha gave simple instructions for Right Intention: practice nonharming and nonclinging. In some sense, his entire teachings—the whole of the Dharma—are contained in these instructions.

With Right Intention, we embark on the next three aspects of the Eightfold Path: Right Speech, the foundation of all skillful relationships; Right Action, which is embodied in the Five Precepts, the Buddhist moral guideposts; and Right Livelihood, the living expression of our wisdom and compassion. When our intention and actions align with the Dharma in this way, our lives tend to make sense, to feel harmonious and integrated. While we will certainly continue to have challenges and difficulties in our lives, we'll be relieved of much of the confusion, conflict, and sense of incompleteness that come when we lack these fundamental guidelines and behaviors.

The last three elements of the Eightfold Path are what most people associate with Buddhism: Right Effort, Right Mindfulness, and Right Concentration. This "mind training" may be what sets Buddhism apart from other religions, philosophies, and practices. These elements allow a stabilizing of the mind and penetrating insight that take us beyond conventional human understanding. It was through the application of these elements of the path that the Buddha was able to have his remarkable breakthrough in consciousness, and he offers us these same tools for our own inner exploration. The promise of awakening that these practices make is what has kept Buddhism alive for millennia, as one master after another, generation after generation, has passed on these teachings.

What is so powerful about these teachings is the opportunity for each of us through our own actions, our own karmic effort, to experience what the Buddha experienced. Rather than an esoteric or mystical tradition, Buddhism is openhanded, freely offered to anyone willing to make the effort. From the first glimmers of truth with Right View, through wise intentions, actions, and meditative practices, each of us can take the actions that bring freedom, joy, and happiness. This is the promise of the Buddha, the simple results of the Law of Karma.

Values

When I talk about integrating values and behavior, in some ways, I don't feel that I need to be terribly prescriptive. I trust that most people have an inner moral compass. The issue for addicts isn't that we don't have this kind of conscience, but that we don't listen to it, or we drown it out with booze and drugs. Buddhism's Five Precepts embody basic moral guidelines: not to kill, not to steal, not to harm others with our sexual behavior, not to lie, and not to use intoxicants. Other than the precept on intoxicants, these are pretty common to most religions. The problem for addicts is that when we break the last precept by getting intoxicated, we tend to break the others. So getting clean and sober takes us a long way toward bringing our behavior in line with our values.

Twelve Step values include honesty, faith, acceptance, commitment, responsibility, letting go, nonharming, peace, and service.

Buddhism offers other values like compassion, nonviolence, interdependence, generosity, forgiveness, and mindfulness. As we progress in recovery and deepen our awareness, these spiritual values can come more to the forefront. In terms of "walking the talk," these are more challenging values to live up to because they aren't just behaviors we can change, but are based in attitudes, conditioning, and habitual reactions that have to be seen, addressed, engaged, and let go. Much of this work falls under the realm of inner life, which I'll address later. But for now, you might reflect on your own inner and outer values.

REFLECTION **Your Values**

Take some time to consider your life's guiding principles and values. How committed are you to the Five Precepts? Which principles of recovery inspire you? Which principles of Buddhism?

Once you are clear on your key values, ask yourself which of these you are fulfilling and which you are not. Consider making a commitment or vow to live by your highest values. ∎

Working with the Twelve Steps

In my years of recovery, I've seen many people who seemed to be confused about the meaning of the Twelve Steps. This is one of the reasons I began to use Buddhist teachings as a way to understand the Steps. The language of Western Buddhism is, for many people, more accessible than the language of middle-twentieth-century American religion that the Steps and Twelve Step literature use. But, even beyond trying to bring a Buddhist understanding to the Steps, I've wanted to draw out the fundamental underlying process that both paths describe—the essential elements of a spiritual journey. I'd like to sketch out this journey and the related aspects of Buddhism and the Twelve Steps.

THE TWELVE STEPS OF ALCOHOLICS ANONYMOUS

1. We admitted we were powerless over alcohol—that our lives had become unmanageable.

2. Came to believe that a Power greater than ourselves could restore us to sanity.

3. Made a decision to turn our will and our lives over to the care of God, *as we understood Him.*

4. Made a searching and fearless moral inventory of ourselves.

5. Admitted to God, to ourselves, and to another human being the exact nature of our wrongs.

6. Were entirely ready to have God remove all these defects of character.

7. Humbly asked Him to remove our shortcomings.

8. Made a list of all persons we had harmed, and became willing to make amends to them all.

9. Made direct amends to such people wherever possible, except when to do so would injure them or others.

10. Continued to take personal inventory, and when we were wrong promptly admitted it.

11. Sought through prayer and meditation to improve our conscious contact with God, *as we understood Him,* praying only for knowledge of His will for us and the power to carry that out.

12. Having had a spiritual awakening as the result of these Steps, we tried to carry this message to alcoholics, and to practice these principles in all our affairs.

The Wake Up Call

The beginning of any inner work is the disquieting sense that something is wrong, either in our own lives or in the way people around us live. This may come as a mild discomfort with our corporate job and lead to our reading a spiritual book we wouldn't have been interested in before; maybe we then take a yoga or meditation class, and start to get in touch with a part of ourselves long suppressed. For addicts, the realization that something's wrong usually comes in a much more dramatic fashion: waking up in jail, getting a divorce petition, losing a job, or getting sick. "Hitting bottom" may also be less dramatic, but is always a turning point. What's important isn't so much the nature of the problem that we wake up to, but our response to it. The Buddha's moment of waking up was existential, realizing that everything around him was subject to decay and death and seeing the pointlessness of pursuing a life of pleasure that could never bring satisfaction. Bill Wilson, the cofounder of Alcoholics Anonymous, got his wakeup call in a blinding flash of insight while detoxing in a hospital bed.

What these two paths share, then, is the realization that the way we are living doesn't work. In the Twelve Step world, we call this "coming out of denial"; in Buddhism, it's called "Right View"—dispelling ignorance or delusion. The addict then sees that their relationship to the addictive drug or behavior is what is causing them suffering; the Buddhist sees the more general truth that clinging to anything is what is causing suffering.

Many people struggle with the term *powerless* in Step One or with the idea that their lives are "unmanageable," and while I think those terms can be explained in useful ways (which I've tried to do in my other books), what's important isn't the specifics of language, but the overriding point: things need to change. In the language of the spiritual journey, Step One and the first Noble Truth are "the wake-up call." Much more than questioning, "Am I really an addict?" or, "Do I really have to go to those meetings?", we need to find a way to respond to this call. That's the beginning of the spiritual journey.

There Is a Way

Once we've accepted that we need to face our problems and begin the process of change, we are faced with two questions: "Can I do it?" and "Is there a way?" Many people struggle with one or both of these questions. People come to a meditation class and find that no matter how hard they try, they can't seem to keep their attention on the breath, the simple instruction the teacher is giving. In the recovery world, people often relapse, and this failure triggers doubt in their capacity to stay in recovery. Others question the whole process they see laid out in the Twelve Steps or at a treatment center. In the Buddhist world, people often struggle with the teachings on suffering or the idea of "no-self."

This, then, is the problem of faith: if we don't believe in ourselves or we don't believe in the process, at least enough to try it, we won't engage in the necessary work, and that belief will be a self-fulfilling prophecy—without some trust or faith, in ourselves and the process, we have very little chance of success. This doesn't mean we have to fully embrace the process, just that we have to have enough trust to get started.

This is why Step Two says, "We came to believe that a Power greater than ourselves could restore us to sanity," and why the third Noble Truth essentially says, "If clinging causes suffering, then it is possible to end suffering by ending clinging"—that is, by letting go. Both of these statements are reassuring us that, despite whatever problem we have encountered, there is the possibility of freedom, of ending suffering. In fact, embedded in the problem is this potential.

In the Twelve Step world, this is where the question—and problem—of God arises. When I first read this Step, I thought it meant, "If you just believe in God, He'll fix you." That's not at all how I see the Step anymore; now I believe that the Step is about hope and the potential for change. Many addicts lose hope, and recovery is partly the delicate rebuilding of this belief in life. The language of *God* and *Higher Power* is simply the cultural and religious reference point that the early Twelve Step members had for understanding this process. A broad reading of the Twelve Step literature reveals that there was a wide range of ideas about God and spirituality in these members, but that what they agreed on was the need for *some kind* of spiritual connection in order to recover, not necessarily a belief in a specific God. In fact, one early piece of AA writing, which came out of AA cofounder Dr. Bob Smith's thinking, said that the Eightfold Path of Buddhism could be a substitute for the Twelve Steps. Such statements might come as a shock to those who believe the founders took a strictly Christian view of religion and spirituality. The "Akron Pamphlets," where this statement is found, say, "It would be nice if God were a stately old gentleman, benign, with a long gray beard, clothed in flowing white gown. . . . But unfortunately, it's not as simple as that." So, apparently, even the people who wrote the AA literature didn't believe in a magical version of God.

The correlation between Step Two and the third Noble Truth points to the shared understanding that before engaging in a new way of living, there must be some degree of confidence in the path.

Entering the Stream

Once we've seen the problem and believe that there is a path, we now engage fully in the recovery process—or in Buddhist terms, in working toward freedom through the Eightfold Path. By cultivating the three elements of the Buddhist path—morality, meditation, and wisdom—we create the conditions for letting go, the cure for suffering.

The Twelve Step way may not seem quite so clear, and presents problems for people oriented to a nontheistic way of viewing the world. Step Three tells us to turn our lives over to God, with the parenthetical comment that we can define that God for ourselves. Again, this can sound essentially like a religious statement suggesting that the whole process is faith based. But I think that's a superficial reading. What's happening here is what's called in Buddhism "Taking Refuge." Step Three is reminding us that our addictive behavior has been based in self-centered pleasure seeking and ego gratification, and that we need to find more skillful motivations for our actions. "Turning our will and our lives over to God" means that we are going to start to live by another set of values, values of nonharming, generosity, and kindness. "God" in this sense just stands for morality and wisdom.

The Eightfold Path, as the "Akron Pamphlets" suggest, presents a perfect way to do this Step. It gives us clear instructions about how to harmonize with the Law of Karma, how to move our lives forward in positive ways, to get along in the world without harming others or ourselves.

Step Three is, for me, the key to the program, and contains many elements. One underlying theme of the Step is acceptance—not struggling with the world or with ourselves. The Serenity Prayer, often recited at Twelve Step meetings, points to this aspect of the Step. The Buddhist corollary to acceptance is equanimity, a clear-eyed and peaceful awareness of what is that contains both wisdom and compassion. Many people in recovery find that the serenity and equanimity that come with working this Step are the beginning of true happiness in recovery.

The Examined Life

The spiritual journey now circles back, with the understanding that we can't move forward if we don't have some understanding of the past. Step Four begins a process of self-examination called "inventory." In Buddhism, we find that the practice of meditation is inherently one of self-examination. What Step Four implies is that even with the commitment to change that we make in Step Three, changing the habits of a lifetime isn't easy. For anyone who has sat down to meditate and found themselves lost in their usual preoccupations instead of following the breath, this is self-evident.

Step Four prods you to look at the truth of your habitual ways of acting, especially the ways you have harmed others. This is a kind of inventory of past karma. If we are meditating just to feel good or to have some special spiritual moment, we are likely to avoid the kind of difficult investigation that inventory involves. In my early practice, before I got sober, I never really looked at my behavior in this way, and so I never really went deeply into the truth of how harmful my behaviors were, both to myself and to others.

Step Five tells us to share this truth with another. This has several purposes, among them making sure that we don't hide or keep secret the behaviors we are ashamed of. In the sharing, the shame is often dispelled. Another purpose of the sharing is to get some perspective. When another addict hears our story, the response is usually something like, "I've heard worse," or even, "I've done worse." This helps the person who is sharing to see that their behavior probably wasn't as bad or outside the norm as they imagined. One of the risks of a silent meditation practice is that we never expose ourselves to others. In my teaching, I try to emphasize the importance of people connecting with others in the *sangha,* the Buddhist community, and being open about who they are, both the good and the not-so-good.

Letting Go

Letting go is the heart of any spiritual journey—letting go of destructive habits, letting go of clinging to people and things, and letting go of ego, self-centeredness, and attachment to identity. Step Six begins the process of change by setting our intention. The Buddha tells us that karma is fueled by intention, and the Steps seem to acknowledge that truth in various ways. We can say that much of our spiritual practice is preparing the ground for letting go to happen.

With Step Seven, we begin to "beseech the law of karma with action, not merely with words." Although this Step seems to say that what we're supposed to do is just ask God to "remove our shortcomings," clearly a prayer or some words won't change us. Step Seven is something that is done on a regular basis by anyone on a spiritual path. It is the ongoing effort to let go of craving and clinging and to cultivate positive actions in the form of thoughts, words, and deeds. This is how we live our spiritual principles. It can include the range of spiritual, psychological, and somatic healing practices.

Healing the Past

For the spiritual journey to be complete, we must come to some peace with those in our family and community. While this healing may never be total, the effort to bring harmony is vital to developing a peaceful heart. Step Eight tells you that you must be honest about exactly who you hurt. Another act of intention, Step Eight brings us directly into the interpersonal realm and begins the process of healing our relationships by looking clearly at who we harmed. When we do the Buddhist practice of *metta,* or lovingkindness, we make a similar list.

With Step Nine, you make the direct effort to heal past harms. Making amends has a powerfully humbling effect—it's the final act of honesty that began with Step One and deepened in Steps Four and Five. This humbling is a vital part of Step work, helping us to let go of ego and accept ourselves as simply human. As the AA Big Book shows in the section commonly called "The Promises," which appears at Step Nine, the implications and results of taking this important Step may be far beyond the obvious healing of relationships. Equally important as the specific amends is the ongoing commitment to become transparent, humble, and ready to admit our failings that this Step encourages.

Living the Life of the Spirit

In the traditional arc of the spiritual journey, the resolution is a coming home. That coming home is really about coming home to ourselves, settling into a new, healthier, wiser, and more caring identity.

The last three Steps bring us into the realm of "maintenance," or living the program/practice. The Steps should never be thought of as just a bunch of actions to get through, but rather understood to encompass a way of living.

Step Ten acknowledges that despite all our work, many of us find that habits of reactivity, judgment, and resentment persist in recovery. This Step reminds us of the importance of being honest about these behaviors when they crop up again. A major cause for relapse and spiritual backsliding is our sense that now that we're sober we're supposed to be "good." Shame and guilt over not living up to our own standards can make it hard to be honest about the fact that we still aren't perfect. If we can live with and accept our own imperfection, we'll have a much easier time of it. This Step encourages us to do just that.

In a sense, then, this brings us back to Step One, showing the circularity or spiral form of spiritual growth. Rather than being on a ladder or upward arc, we cycle up, around, and back, over and over, each time finding ourselves in a different part of the spiral, and yet faced with similar challenges to be honest, persistent, and engaged with the latest challenge.

Step Eleven, by encouraging prayer and meditation, brings forward the importance of a spiritual practice. While much Step work is about skillful behavior, now we attend more to the inner life. Until this Step is fully engaged, few will reap the true benefits of peace, clarity, and insight that recovery promises. We can see that this Step gives us the most direct connection to Buddhism. It is when people begin to get serious about meditation in their recovery that they often start to explore the Buddhist practices.

The sense of connection that's implied in the phrase "conscious contact" links us to the present moment as well as to the world around us. The inner looking and reflection of meditation have the effect of bringing the outer world alive for us.

Step Eleven talks again about power, the power that's unleashed by letting go of ego and craving and seeking the highest forms of wisdom and guidance.

So in many ways it is this Step that fulfills the promise of recovery and spiritual work. If our program is solely focused on external behaviors and internal flaws, we are missing a great deal of what recovery has to offer—indeed, of what life has to offer. In a culture that's so materially and externally focused, it's a huge challenge for many of us to engage this inner path. Without it, though, our recovery rests on shaky ground.

Step Twelve comprises three elements: spiritual awakening, service to others, and commitment to a life of recovery and spiritual principles. Each of these elements is found in Buddhism as well. The Buddha's ultimate effort was to help us to wake up, to taste the freedom of enlightenment; his path, and that of his followers, culminates in the realization that self-seeking is fruitless and that the skillful response to a spiritual awakening is to help others to attain the same breakthrough; finally, there can be no loopholes, no excuses or exceptions to our commitment—otherwise we risk losing what we have gained.

Spiritual awakening can be understood in many different ways, ranging from the dramatic experience of enlightenment that the Buddha embodies to the simple realization that life lived as an addict is a dead end. I believe that enlightenment as promised by the Buddha is available to each of us, but its attainment requires a level of commitment that few can achieve. This is why, while there may be millions of Westerners who follow Buddhist teachings and practices, few have taken ordination as monastics, the ultimate commitment to the Buddhist path. Nonetheless, our spiritual journey provides many moments of insight, connection, and opening, many experiences of compassion, forgiveness, and love, all of which are awakenings. The wonderful thing about this path is that it always seems to provide more opportunities to grow and deepen our understanding.

The spirit of service that this Step encourages and that the Buddha expressed is well known to be a route out of suffering. When we focus on others, we stop obsessing about our own problems. As Ajahn Sumedho, the revered American monk, says, "Whenever I think about myself I get depressed." Helping others frees us from this quagmire as well as giving us a positive experience to reflect on.

The final admonition of the Step, to live our recovery in every aspect of our lives, puts a period on the path. When the Buddha talks about mindfulness, he says the same thing: that every action should be engaged with mindfulness. Spiritual practice and growth, then, aren't about rituals or special experiences, nor about achieving something or looking good, but about how we meet this moment, this person, this day, about staying present, openhearted, and honest, living the principles right now.

The Twelve Steps and Happiness

Since this book is supposed to be about finding happiness in recovery, let me briefly show how I think the Steps themselves contain and bring happiness.

Step One. As I described in the "Giving Up" section earlier in this chapter, there can be great joy in just stopping. Letting go of our addiction is a huge relief. In spiritual terms, this is surrender, an element of every spiritual tradition that contains an aspect of joy, relief, and devotion.

Step Two. There is great comfort in the realization that we aren't alone, that there is help, and that we can heal our lifelong suffering.

Step Three. With this Step comes the beginnings of serenity and clarity. Now we see that we are on our path and that we're going to be okay. Another, deeper surrender brings a level of spiritual peace that many of us had never experienced.

Step Four. Painful as it can be to look at our past mistakes, the sense that we are really on our way to recovery gives momentum and excitement to the process. While we may feel bad about what we did in the past, we can see that we are no longer engaged in these behaviors and that our past doesn't define or limit us.

Step Five. There can be great relief and joy at unburdening ourselves of our secrets and shame. When these secrets are shared with a skillful and compassionate sponsor or other spiritual friend, the reflection they give brings our past into perspective and shows us that, while we may have done some bad things, we were not bad people. Essentially, we were just confused and struggling human beings who made the same mistakes that many, if not most, humans make.

Bill Wilson says that when we complete this Step, "We feel we are on the Broad Highway, walking hand in hand with the Spirit of the Universe." This beautiful image brings to life the sense of freedom that can come from sharing our inventory.

Step Six. At this point, we are moving away from the past contained in our inventory and toward a future of healing. Again, the momentum of the Steps seems to be accumulating, and by now we're fully committed and engaged in the process. The sense of potential for a new, exciting, and fulfilling life overtakes us and brings real joy.

Step Seven. By taking the actions we know will continue to help us to heal and grow, we are now living the Steps and the Eightfold Path. No longer faking it or just doing what we're supposed to, by the time we engage this Step, most of us feel a great sense of possibility and even inevitability that our life is finally turning around.

Step Eight. While it can be agonizing to review the list of those we both loved and resented (who were sometimes the same people), we can feel confident that "the finish line" is in sight—that the journey through our painful past is nearing its resolution. At this point, our commitment to honesty is so total that we might even feel a sense of freedom in simply admitting the truth of this list.

Step Nine. Certainly making amends is a difficult and sometimes painful process, but most of us have had remarkable moments of freedom and joy when our amends were accepted. On the other hand, a difficult amends that isn't received so kindly helps us to deepen our acceptance, both of the person we harmed and of our lack of control over others. We know within ourselves that we truly regret our actions and that we have changed. If others can't see and accept that, it is not our responsibility.

Step Ten. It brings a great sense of safety to know that we are not accumulating piles of new bad karma. When we stay honest and current, we don't carry around a burden of guilt. At this point, there can also be a sense of letting go around protecting the self. The ego becomes less vulnerable because we don't see it as representing something so real or important.

Step Eleven. For many, this is one of the most joyful of all the Steps. As our spiritual life deepens, we begin to touch the deeper forms of happiness, unrelated to the material world. The depth of peace accessible through meditation can introduce us to an entirely different realm of existence. The sense of connection and being at home in the world allows us to live fully and let go completely.

Step Twelve. Certainly a spiritual awakening, in whatever form it takes, is a cause for joy and celebration. The service that arises from that awakening helps us to stop focusing on our own concerns and to experience the joy of giving. Finally, the clarity and safety derived from living our principles fully complete the sense of peace, joy, and fulfillment that the Steps promise.

PEOPLE WHO NEED PEOPLE

satisfying interpersonal relationships

Our relationships with others may be the most important external influence on our happiness. While growing up, it's our family that is so important for most of us; later on, our friends, lovers, partners, and children take on a central role in our lives; along the way, spiritual community, teachers, and healers are vital to how our lives unfold. No one can do the Twelve Steps for us; no one can meditate in our place. But Buddhist practice and Twelve Step work both depend on the help and support of others. Recovery and spiritual growth are collaborative efforts. While we can't expect others to make us happy, we have to learn to navigate these many relationships skillfully to have a chance at contentment and joy.

Happiness and Spiritual Community

One of the common observations about addicts is that we like to isolate, to withdraw from the world and find refuge in our drug of choice. By the time I had become addicted to marijuana, as a poor musician, I became very stingy with my pot. When the band took a break, I'd sneak out of the club, smoke a carefully measured bowl, and come back in time for the next set, all ready to play. At that stage, I felt no need to socialize around my pot smoking. It wasn't about that; it was about being high, period.

One of the symptoms of alcoholism and drug addiction is drinking or using alone. Most normal drinkers have a couple of glasses of wine at a party or a beer after work with the guys or gals. They don't slam back three or four drinks *before* they meet up with their friends, as I would do, just so they don't have to *appear* to be drinking a lot.

When we're not isolating, we tend to see other people as resources to exploit, potential sexual partners, or sources of money or favors. Sharing and community are alien to us because they mean giving, and we're all about getting.

One of the principles of happiness is that it comes from giving, not getting, so the addictive strategy of selfishness only leads to disappointment and frustration, not happiness.

The Buddha famously says that "noble friends and noble conversations are the whole of the holy life." When I first heard this teaching, I was surprised because I'd always thought that meditation was the most important aspect of Buddhism. It's interesting, though, that the Buddha makes the connection between our relationships and our spiritual growth. He says that to become enlightened we need to act on skillful values, and that if we live around people who have good values and skillful behavior, we will tend to act on the same positive values; he says that we need to hear the Dharma, and that if we live around other people who want to hear the Dharma, we will hear it; he says that we need to make wise effort, and that if we are involved with other people who are making wise effort, we will as well. All of this is to show the importance of community in our spiritual growth.

Community is the very basis of Twelve Step work, so people who have been a part of that program understand this. They say it's hard to get clean and sober alone, and that was my experience. Most of us tried to do it alone, or at least to manage our using alone, and failed repeatedly.

It's hard as well to learn to meditate or to sustain a meditation practice alone. Without a teacher, it's very tough to learn the nuances of meditation. Without a sangha of support, it's hard to keep showing up on your cushion. Oftentimes at the end of my retreats, people who don't live near any Buddhist centers ask how they can sustain their practice. I usually wind up suggesting they try to find some like-minded people to meditate with and maybe form a Buddhist recovery group.

The Buddhist recovery movement now tries to draw on the traditional Twelve Step meeting format, blending this with the typical Buddhist meditation group so that the hybrid brings a balance of quiet contemplation and group support. This meeting form mirrors the connections I've been trying to make between Buddhism and the Twelve Steps.

Meetings of any kind, whether Buddhist or Twelve Step or something else, are a good way to get us out of isolation. There's no risk of rejection or abandonment as in a friendship or romance, and there isn't necessarily any emotional commitment. In those senses, going to meetings can be the baby steps for a newcomer in recovery to start developing healthy relationships. The meetings themselves are safely structured, so that, if we want, we can just sit and listen, or we can share without fear of interruption, judgment, or conflict. As we grow in recovery, we can start to connect with the fellowship or sangha outside the confines of the meeting. In this way, many people have developed new relationships and connections that have become the social foundation of their lives. We can then start to carry the things we learn in this community out into other relationships.

The first time I went to a Twelve Step meeting it was to support a woman I was seeing as she tried to kick cocaine. I hadn't yet figured out that I too had a problem, but looking back, it's not surprising how comfortable I felt there. The stories of addiction were very familiar. What struck me most, though, was the laughter and energy. People were excited and happy to be there—that is to say, it was a typical Twelve Step meeting.

Later, after I got sober, I loved hearing the story that one woman in my home group told about a newcomer who'd told the woman that she wasn't sure she was an alcoholic. "Oh, be one. It's fun!" said my friend. This story never failed to get big laughs—because it's true. Of course, the laughter is over the irony of how true it is. No one who comes to a meeting for the first time is coming to have fun. But that's what we find—at least some of the time.

Many addicts have painful family histories, and many of us struggle to figure out how to create healthy intimate relationships. One place where it can be a little safer to connect is in our spiritual community. A healthy sangha or fellowship is warm, accepting, and friendly. It allows for our quirks and difficult qualities. And it supports us as we try to grow.

In community, we can find opportunities for service, one of the most reliable sources of happiness. Service is a given in the Twelve Step world and built into Step Twelve, which tells us that once we have achieved some spiritual growth, we need to "carry the message" to others who face the same challenges we once did. While this may sound altruistic, the founders of AA were very clear that they were helping other drunks *to keep themselves sober.* They had discovered that helping others took their minds off their own problems, gave them a positive feeling about themselves, and kept them in touch with the realities of active addiction. Virtually every spiritual or religious system encourages service. Buddhism, with its emphasis on compassion and selflessness, certainly follows this model. For me, becoming part of a community and learning to be of service wasn't easy.

I grew up in an insular family; with four older brothers, I didn't have to go anywhere to have social contact. We were popular in our way, but never had to reach out or enter unfamiliar social situations. I never went to camp, joined the Boy Scouts, or even socialized with people outside my immediate circle. When I became a musician, it gave me both a built-in community—the band—and a way of being involved with social groups without really interacting. I could be up on stage getting attention and ego gratification, but never really connecting with others.

When it came time for me to join a Twelve Step group, the idea was completely alien. Although I knew that I needed help, I didn't want to join anything. However, I'd failed often enough on my own to be skeptical of my own capacity to stay clean and sober. So I was afraid, maybe even superstitious, about trying to do it alone. My solution for the first year of my sobriety was to stay in the back of the room, literally. I would often just stand by the door and listen to the speaker or the people sharing. I laughed, I learned, and I left before anyone could say hello, shake my hand, or give me their phone number. As it says in the Twelve Step literature, "Half measures availed us nothing." Though I wouldn't go so far as to say that this level of commitment was worthless, I was far from getting the full benefit of recovery.

At a certain point, I decided that actually becoming a member of the Twelve Step groups I was attending might help with the persistent loneliness I felt. Finally, after a whole year sober, I actually started to do what was suggested (yes, I'm a slow learner). I went to meetings every day, talked to people, exchanged phone numbers, and finally, asked someone to sponsor me.

I started working the Steps, writing inventory, making amends, and finally, practicing Step Twelve. My sponsor suggested that I take a service position at a meeting, so I volunteered to be a cleanup person, sweeping the floor of the social room in the church where I attended a Thursday morning meeting. The first thing I discovered was that when you help a group, you meet people. The second thing I learned was that meeting people made me feel like part of the group. The third thing I learned was that feeling like a part of the group felt really good. (Like I said, I'm a slow learner.)

Something clicked for me then, and my whole attitude changed. I started to volunteer to do service at other meetings. When I got an office job, I started to feel that I was being of service there, as well as part of a work community. Eventually, I would bring this attitude to my Buddhist practice and start doing service there as well. And all of this brought real happiness and a sense of connection.

In the Twelve Step world, we talk about community as fellowship; in the Buddhist world, it's sangha. Some Twelve Steppers call the fellowship their "Higher Power." In this sense, people turn to the group as a place of wisdom, support, love, and connection. They bring their problems to the group and listen for answers; they bring their broken hearts to the group and get held in love; they bring their loneliness and find joy and friendship. If "God is Love," then the group can certainly be a Higher Power. On perhaps a more practical level, turning to the group for this kind of support and guidance means trying not to follow your own negative impulses, listening to outer voices instead of inner ones. This can take the form of simply going to a meeting and hearing others speak; many times, I've discovered that when I go to a meeting with something on my mind, somehow that exact subject gets addressed in the meeting. It also can take the form of one-on-one connection, asking someone for help or guidance, be they a friend or sponsor. Finally, turning it over to the group can also mean helping someone else. This comes back to the idea of service as healing. Anyone who's been around the Twelve Step world for very long—and this has happened to me innumerable times—knows how you can get to a meeting caught up in your own problem du jour and wind up listening to someone else's problem after the meeting, forgetting all about yourself, and walking away feeling lighter, happier, and somehow relieved of your anxiety or concerns. This is the power of connection.

In a Buddhist community, the support and connection are equally important. Meditation practice is challenging and can feel isolating, so it's important to have others with whom we share our experiences. Further, as we go deeper into dharma study, we may find ourselves alienated from the materialism around us and need support from others who likewise question the goals of accumulation and pleasure seeking. Our mainstream culture often seems to value things that are directly in opposition to Buddhist teachings on compassion and renunciation, so we need to have a community that shares our values and supports us in trying to live by these principles.

In some ways, it's more difficult to connect in the Buddhist community because so much of our practice is in silence. Besides that, while a Twelve Step meeting allows people to be completely open and honest, the spiritual nature and setting of Buddhist gatherings can encourage a wish to conceal our darker secrets, as we try to look good or live up to some image of perfection we see embodied in the Buddha and our teachers. This is one reason why in my own teaching I try to break down projections and expectations.

The point of all this is that being part of community makes you happy. I don't think I've ever left a meeting or a meditation group feeling worse than when I arrived. When we are feeling blue, it can seem like a big effort or burden to have to leave the house and go join a group. Maybe you've had a long day or you're depressed, anxious, resentful, or stressed. Attending a group feels pointless, and you'd rather just stay home with your microwave dinner and TV set. But we all know that stewing in our problems never solves them, that passivity in the face of distress only deepens the suffering.

What Is Love?

I often teach a class on Buddhism at a local college for their "Jan Term," when students take just one course for the month of January, four days a week. I teach a little about Buddhist history and take them through the basic teachings, but mostly I emphasize learning meditation. At a certain point, I introduce the concept of metta (lovingkindness), the unconditional love that the Buddha encouraged us to practice. Buddhist teachers have adapted the idea of sharing and spreading lovingkindness into a formal meditation practice. I teach the students this practice in the traditional way, asking them to start by thinking of someone who is easy to love, sending that person love, and then starting to send love to themselves. Next we send love to our family and friends; then we move on to a "neutral" person and then a "difficult" person; and finally we radiate love to all beings. What I've found is that these college kids often just hang out sending love to family and friends. They really don't take on the more difficult aspects of the practice—working with the neutral, and especially the difficult, person.

I've begun to suspect that this is actually very common. A couple decades ago, lovingkindness started to move to the forefront of practices in the *vipassana* world (*vipassana* is the Buddhist term for mindfulness meditation). With the publication of Sharon Salzberg's classic *Lovingkindness: The Revolutionary Art of Happiness,* and then a new emphasis by many teachers on this practice, lovingkindness seemed to become an alternative to traditional insight meditation. Retreats that focused exclusively on lovingkindness were offered, and certain teachers began to specialize in the practice. In some ways, I think this was a welcome balance to the somewhat-dry insight practices. But, in another way, I suspect that the practice was being used in the way my college students did, as a sort of palliative or feel-good practice.

Now, since I'm supposed to be writing a book about cultivating happiness, you might ask why I would complain about people feeling good. And it's certainly not that I don't want people to enjoy their meditation, because I do; in fact, I think it's important to enjoy meditation. But simply focusing on things that make you feel good for a few minutes isn't happiness—or meditation. As I think we all know, long-term happiness often involves short-term discomfort. If we are using meditation as an escape or a quick fix, we're not working toward true happiness. Happiness in meditation arises out of calm, concentration, and insight, and that's a process. That process doesn't avoid difficult feelings (or difficult people); it is open to life as it is, to the complexities of the heart and mind. And it develops a balance of heart and mind that is nonreactive, compassionate, and wise. The lovingkindness practice in its full form does just this. It deepens calm, concentration, and insight, and it trains the heart/mind to be equanimous, caring, clear-eyed, and wise.

The love that the Buddha is talking about is universal, unconditional love. The Metta Sutta, the original discourse the Buddha gave on lovingkindness, tells us to cherish every living being, to radiate kindness over the entire world. In another *sutta,* the Buddha says that if someone were sawing off our limbs and a thought of ill will arose, we wouldn't be practicing his path. This is an awfully high standard, but the Buddha had high standards. And obviously, this teaching isn't about just feeling good; it's about something much deeper and more profound than that. The love the Buddha is talking about almost bears no relation to our culture's use of the term. In fact, the Buddha often refers to "non-ill-will" rather than love. He says this, for one thing, because the Buddhist understanding is that when we remove or let go of ill will, love is the natural result; it's already there, just waiting to be exposed. I think he also says this for the same reason he talks about "nonclinging" and uses negative terms in many other contexts—because it leaves you nothing to hold on to. When someone says "love," we get a picture in our mind that we can cling to. When someone says "non-ill-will," there's nothing to cling to. This was one of the Buddha's brilliant rhetorical strategies: his way of expressing himself in and of itself encouraged letting go, the precise result he was trying to achieve in his teaching.

Returning to the question of happiness, it is unconditional, universal love that brings true happiness. The Buddha points out on multiple occasions the limits of conditional love, how having expectations of others or attachment to them leads to disappointment, loss, and suffering; he emphasizes the destructive qualities of aversion and hatred, how rejecting or disparaging people only brings us more agitation and stress. But when there is open, free-flowing love, there are none of these downfalls. Practicing sending love to neutral and difficult people helps us to discover this unconditional love, as it challenges us to get past our limited, self-centered feelings about people and focus instead on our shared human longing for happiness. When we look on the world with caring, compassion, appreciation, and equanimity—the four Brahmaviharas—we are peaceful and happy. And it's these qualities that the lovingkindness practices cultivate in us.

Of course, we can't all be Buddhas. Most (all?) of us have limits to our capacity for love, and we feel attachment to those we do love. I don't know what the Buddha's intention was in setting such high standards, but we do discover in the suttas that as he got old and many of the companions he had practiced and lived with for so many years started to die off, he was sad. So was he attached to his friends? I suppose I hope so, because that just makes the Buddha more human. In any case, I don't think it's helpful to think that we should somehow not feel attachment to our children, partner, or friends. Rather, what I take from the Buddha's teaching is that I need to be realistic: if I am attached, there will be suffering. But, as far as I'm concerned, that's okay. Dukkha, the pain of loss and discontent, is part of life; to think we can avoid it is to live in a dream. The teachings help us not to be confused: we see the connection between cause and effect, and perhaps we can develop some equanimity around that.

As my daughter grows up, I feel the loss of her childhood; as I grow older, I feel the sadness of losing my own youth; as my friends die, I mourn. But none of this means that I am unhappy. What I believe causes unhappiness is confusion and struggle. If I didn't understand my sadness or why everything is changing, that would be painful; if I couldn't fundamentally accept these changes, that would be troubling. The Dharma gives me a clear way to understand and hold these truths. Love is to be treasured here and now. Take joy, and let go.

Intimacy, Sex, and Romantic Love

I realize that asking the question "What is love?" then going on about lovingkindness without mentioning sex or romance is a bit disingenuous of me. In our culture, the term *love* first and foremost refers to romantic love, and romance, according to our cultural definition, includes sex.

Ajahn Amaro, the English Theravadan monk, makes the point that our culture views falling in love somewhat the way that Buddhists view enlightenment: as the ultimate spiritual experience. When we fall in love, we are supposed to have achieved total fulfillment and "live happily ever after." Shakespeare's comedies invariably end with marriage, as do many of our romantic-comedy movies. The message is: "There's really nothing more to achieve in life. The main story is over. From here on, everything will be just fine and dandy."

Unfortunately, that is a fairy tale.

Our belief in this narrative just shows the great power of the survival instinct, since what it's really expressing is the imperative to procreate, which, once achieved, fulfills our genetic destiny and evolutionary purpose. Our genes don't really care what happens after that, as long as they've been replicated. To me, our blind acceptance of this idea of romantic love as life's highest achievement just shows the superficiality of most humans' thinking. One doesn't have to look far to see the absolute emptiness of this promise.

Let's start by looking at this idea from the Buddhist perspective. The Buddha was not a fan of romantic love because it essentially fulfills the exact requirements of the cause of suffering: it's all about craving and attachment, and because it's based on impermanent feelings, it has no lasting power. The state of mind called "in love" is wonderful, joyful, and brief. Most people find that they either fall out of love or move into a less compelling state in six months to a year after the original falling. What happens then, if people truly have a connection, is that they start to form an actual relationship (more on that later).

From the standpoint of addiction, falling in love can actually be dangerous. People who are prone to sex and/or love addiction—and many addicts and alcoholics are—tend to fall into obsession when they become attached in this way. The result is often possessiveness, jealousy, and painful craving. All of this can lead to stalking, violence, and even murder as we see every day (if we happen to follow such stories in the media). Barring such extremes, some of the typical symptoms of falling in love include ignoring your friends, deluded fantasies, and irrational decisions. We're lucky if we survive such an experience with our lives intact.

Okay, so maybe I'm exaggerating a little. But I'm trying to make a point: falling in love isn't love.

Love is caring for others; love is giving; love is kindness. And, yes, love is also a feeling. But feelings are remarkably fickle, so a better indicator of love is our actions. When we say that we want love, what exactly are we saying? We tend to think that other people can give us love, but is that really true? Have you ever had someone you weren't attracted to plead their undying love to you? Did that feel like love? Probably not. No, love doesn't come from others; it comes from within us. That is why (or is at least one reason why) we practice lovingkindness meditation: to see that we can actually create love within ourselves for ourselves. What a gift! And how different that idea is from the idea of searching for love.

So if this falling-in-love thing isn't the answer to finding happiness, what about after the thrill has worn off? When I was about two years sober, my Twelve Step friends were passing around a cassette tape of Terry Gorski, a well-known addiction counselor and specialist in relapse prevention and codependency, speaking at a Twelve Step convention. On the tape, Gorski talked about addictive relationships and how to avoid them. He talked about the rush of meeting someone who really turned you on, and said that if that happened you should turn around and walk the other way, because inevitably this was the person who was going to set off all your addictive tendencies. And, while the sex would be great and you'd be madly, deeply in love for a little while, soon enough the relationship would degenerate into obsessiveness, clinging, and jealousy or a crushing breakup.

What he was saying resonated deeply with me. At thirty-seven years old, I'd followed those cravings and those rushes many times. In fact, as my sponsor told me at the time, my career was chasing women, not making music. That was a low blow, but not entirely inaccurate. I would have said conservatively that I'd been in love four or five times in my life, depending on how you defined being in love. Never had one of these relationships reached a state of equilibrium where I could imagine marriage or long-term commitment. In every one of these relationships, after the initial thrill wore off I'd slept with other women—usually when I was on the road with a band, which I was able to rationalize as not really "cheating," a common musician's dodge. And every time a relationship lasted more than six months and "falling in love" wore off, my engagement in the sexual element sank rapidly. True intimacy never really developed.

Ironically, I have been crueler and more abusive to people I supposedly loved than to anyone else in my life. When alcohol and drugs were combined with immaturity, unreasonable expectations, and selfishness, my behavior, especially in my twenties, was despicable.

So, hearing Gorski say that you essentially shouldn't base a relationship on sexual attraction, I was curious whom I was supposed to go out with. His answer: "boring people." This line got a huge laugh from the convention audience. And it left me curious. What would that really mean?

I got the part about going out with people who triggered obsession. I knew that feeling well, and I understood, from painful experience, the futility of pursuing such obsessions. I was ready to try something different, which in the Twelve Step world is called "having willingness." Step Six says, "We were entirely ready to have God remove all these defects of character." And, while I didn't know about the God part, I understood about the readiness. I knew that I'd never been willing to get sober before I finally did, and I knew that I hadn't been willing to try another approach to relationships until then. So I decided to try it Gorski's way.

I began to take note of the types of attraction I felt for women I encountered. Gradually, I got a sense of what he was talking about when he said "boring people." For me, it meant someone I liked, who I could imagine spending pleasant time with, who wasn't unattractive to me, but who didn't, as he said, set off bells in my head . . . or anywhere else.

I tried going on a date with one or two people like this, and I had a good time. It was very interesting to actually enjoy an evening with a woman, have no sexual contact, and not feel that I necessarily wanted to date her again. It wasn't that I disliked these women or wanted never to see them again; I just felt somewhat neutral. I don't think I'd ever felt that before—I'd always felt either turned on or turned off.

There was one woman in my group of recovery friends who seemed to like me, though, again, I wasn't particularly attracted to her. I just liked her. So I asked her out, and we had a good time. We started to date, and now the next part of Gorski's guidelines became relevant: don't sleep with someone until you know them pretty well. He suggested waiting a certain number of dates or a certain amount of time, something like a couple months. This idea was truly revolutionary for me.

For one thing, my lifestyle of playing in clubs six days a week had meant that I'd almost never actually dated in the conventional sense. I couldn't, because my evenings were mostly filled with work. But now that I was working a day job, I could go out on a weekend evening, not just hook up with someone after a gig. So it felt pleasantly odd to do this normal thing. And then to end a date with just a kiss was odder yet. In the past, if I didn't sleep with someone after being with them once or twice, I figured they didn't like me and there was no point in seeing them again. Now, though, as a new devotee of Gorski's method, I was committed to the plan.

Those weeks were interesting. As we dated, the woman and I became closer and closer, and I found myself becoming more attracted to her sexually. I'd never experienced anything like that. Normally, attraction had been either an on or off switch for me, but now the off switch was changing. When we did eventually sleep together, there was a difference, another level of intimacy I'd never really experienced before. Over time, instead of losing interest sexually, I found myself becoming more attracted to her. This had never happened to me before, either.

We stayed together for two years, and for the first time in my life, I was able to sustain my interest in a woman, not cheat on her, and feel satisfied over a fairly long-term relationship. This was a huge breakthrough, and changed my life. I continued to apply these basic principles to my relationships, and eventually got married.

I'm talking about happiness here, happiness in relationships. And what I'm saying is that for many addicts, normal, healthy intimacy is completely unfamiliar. This means that, like our drinking and using, our dating needs to change as well. We have to be open to new ways of getting involved with people, and we need to make a commitment to change. Our old ways don't and won't work. For many addicts—and for this addict in particular—intimate relationships were at the heart of our recovery. If we don't address our habitual ways of getting involved—romantically, emotionally, sexually—we will miss a big part of recovery. I'm not saying that you have to do it the "Gorski way," but if you have a messy relationship history and addictive tendencies around your sexuality, you are going to have to try something significantly different. And, like the surprise of finding happiness without your drug of choice, I think you will be surprised by the happiness that comes from letting go of your old ideas and behaviors.

This very thought brings us back to the core principle of happiness from a Buddhist viewpoint: it comes from letting go, not from acquiring. Happiness in relationships doesn't come from acquiring great sexual experiences; it comes from letting go of craving and grasping. This seems like a complete paradox, and I'd even say, a contradiction. It's not that we can be involved with a lover without craving and grasping; it's that if we place our desire for sexual pleasure, personal satisfaction, and control before the shared needs of the relationship, we lose the essence of intimacy. In any relationship, there are three elements that must be balanced: the two individuals' needs and the needs of the relationship itself. The self-centered addict overemphasizes his or her own needs; the codependent overemphasizes the needs of the other. Finding a way to take care of ourselves and each other is the great challenge. Love is the guiding principle. And loving someone is not the wish to make them happy or you happy, but to be happy together.

REFLECTION **Relationship Habits**

In this reflection, take time to explore your relationship history. Are there addictive patterns in those relationships? What were your priorities? Did you pursue sexual gratification selfishly? Did you want someone to take care of you? Someone to take care of? What about control? Have you tried to control your partners? Have you been dishonest in your relationships? Withholding of affection or emotion? Cold or grasping? Selfish or self-denying? What other negative behavior patterns keep repeating?

Now consider how to overcome the negative patterns. Would the "Gorski method" help? How about greater honesty? Can you change your expectations? Do you need to work with a therapist either individually or as a couple? What needs to change and how could you change it? ▪

Long-Term Relationship

For many of us, happiness includes a stable, long-term relationship, and that's ultimately what Terry Gorski's advice was meant to make possible. What I started to realize as I tried to change my approach to relationships was that at some point, the same conflicts and blocks came up. As much as I wanted to avoid these issues, I knew that I was never going to go any further in a relationship until I was able to face and deal with them. Whether this challenging stage in relationships was about me and my failings or just an inevitable developmental process in deepening intimacy and involvement, I didn't know. But I did sense that it couldn't be avoided.

There were a few of these blocks. The first, I think, was that my partner's infatuation with me would wear off and she would start to see some of my flaws and point them out. Before I got sober, whenever this happened the fighting began. I'm still not all that good at hearing criticism. But once I went through the inventory and amends process, I at least became capable of admitting that I was sometimes wrong. I began to recognize that my human failings weren't unacceptable. In fact, writing a "searching and fearless moral inventory" and then hearing lots of people's stories in meetings helped me develop compassion for others, which eventually turned into compassion for myself. We're all flawed; we're all imperfect. And we all have the potential to change and grow.

At this stage of a relationship, as the magic wears off and we move into a more functional phase, both people are likely to begin to see things they wish were different in their partner. How we deal with these wishes is critical. If you ask me to please put the toilet seat down after I use it or to remember to take out the garbage, I can do that. Other changes might not be so easy. Obviously, a relationship includes a lot of compromise and negotiation. We learn to distinguish the deal breakers from things that can be accepted, to ask ourselves what's really important to us, what's worth fighting for and what's not.

When you're dating, money tends to be a peripheral issue, but as your lives become intertwined, attitudes about money and earning power can create tremendous conflicts. All of a sudden, the "looks" of our partner's bank account might trump their pretty face. Here we are faced with the larger question of values. While you might have fun with someone, enjoy their company, their sense of humor, and their personality, if you find out that they have vastly different material ambitions, you probably won't last long together.

Then there's the question of children and family. Not too long ago, probably the most important reason to get married was to create a family, having loads of kids. Today, childless couples are common. Even if everything else aligns in a relationship, if this aspect doesn't, the relationship will either end or someone will be unhappy. Then the question of parenting styles comes into play, and can be another source of conflict or harmony.

The sexual aspect of a relationship inevitably changes as well and can block progress. As kids come along, aging changes our bodies, or that part of the relationship simply becomes routine, we're again faced with the question of what we need versus what we want.

Maybe the first thing that has to change if we want to sustain a relationship is our expectations. Addicts like me expect a partner to fix us. We expect great sex on demand, unconditional love, and, essentially, acquiescence to all our demands and wishes. We want someone else to make us happy. Forever.

But maintaining a relationship over time first requires that we adjust our expectations. What is it that I actually want and need from a relationship? This is a very personal question, not one that has a generic answer. Some people need space, others closeness; some need intellectual engagement, others a playmate. We might imagine our perfect partner, and then find someone who fits the bill, only to discover that our "requirements" really weren't what we needed, but rather just a fantasy. I've seen this with people who thought that a fellow Buddhist or fellow recovering alcoholic would be perfect because they would share these important interests, only to find that there were all kinds of conflicts that had nothing to do with these aspects of their lives. It's strange, but there seems to be an odd chemistry that binds people, one that's not so much defined by their outward characteristics or their spiritual résumé.

In my early twenties, I thought that the perfect romance would be with a lead singer. I would play lead guitar; she would sing. We'd travel and perform together, and everything would be great. When I finally realized this ambition, it turned out to be the most tumultuous and dysfunctional relationship of my life.

For the active addict, choices are made so much on impulse and craving that they often wind up in unhealthy relationships. In recovery, these same tendencies can still be there, so as I talked about earlier, many of us have to learn a whole new way of understanding what the purpose of a relationship is and what reasonable expectations are for a partner. These kinds of questions can really use the help of a sponsor, therapist, or spiritual friend to sort out because our old ways of thinking are so unreliable.

Besides expectations, there has to be a willingness to continue to talk, to negotiate, to work together. As someone who often wants to avoid conflict, it's been hard for me to learn to participate in problem-solving with my partner. I tend to be defensive and to interpret slight criticism as a personal attack. This means that I can quickly escalate an offhand comment into a fight. And I can also be very critical and irritable myself, setting off firestorms over minor problems. If I don't have a strong intention to work things out and a willingness to let go, these tendencies can cause deep, ongoing conflicts. My wife and I have been to the brink over such conflicts, and what I think has made us willing to step back from that edge is our strong desire to stay together and to recapture some of the essential connection that we've had for so long.

This kind of realization—that despite all the challenges, we wanted to work things out—isn't necessarily going to be there for every couple. Part of long-term relationships is realizing that sometimes they play themselves out, that two people have changed too much to reconcile, or that they don't want to do the work necessary to stay together. Like everything else, relationships are impermanent, whether they end "when death do us part" or when they simply don't work anymore.

REFLECTION   **What I Want in Relationship**

The exploration of long-term relationships brings up the essential question of what we want. First of all, there is the question of whether we really want to be in a relationship at all. We are indoctrinated from an early age to believe that happiness comes from being married or with a partner, but is that really true for you? If that's what you want, then comes the question of what you want in a partner. Here we have to separate the infantile longings from realistic expectations or needs. Again, we may discover deep conditioning in ourselves that is simply a fantasy.

Here, we have to parse out the difference between our cravings and the things that actually work for us. This is where Gorski's advice about avoiding the person who sets off the bells comes in. Buddhism and the practices it offers help us to see more clearly both what we crave and how we feel. We need to get past the cravings and see how we actually feel around these issues—what will actually makes us happy or fulfill us in the long run versus what we crave or think we need for our immediate satisfaction. Ignorance of this distinction is what drives people to overconsumption, overwork, greed, crime, and all sorts of negative and destructive behaviors. For instance, for most people, having a connection with a partner that is primarily sexual rarely sustains a relationship, even though that might be the overriding craving that controls you. And having a partner who simply provides you with financial security probably won't give you fulfillment either.

If this question is relevant for you right now, take some time to let these questions percolate. Maybe do some writing on the topic and discuss your thoughts with a sponsor or trusted spiritual friend. Try to avoid judging yourself or letting cultural norms dictate your thinking. ▪

Family Karma

How we engage in intimate relationships is deeply conditioned by our family of origin. As we try to develop healthier relationships, we will likely become aware of this conditioning. Sorting out our history with parents and siblings and others is part of moving forward in our own intimacy; understanding that history will also influence our choices and behaviors as we consider starting our own family.

I don't know if I learned much about being in a relationship by watching my parents, but I did see a lot of conflict, struggle, and dissatisfaction. After a couple martinis, my mother would sometimes cry on my shoulder about how she should have married her first beau or that she should have divorced my father. This certainly didn't give me a positive view of marriage or of my own fate. I'm sure a therapist would call this inappropriate boundary crossing for a mother and young son, and there was also the question of whether I even would have existed had my parents not married. Despite all that, my parents stayed married until my father died. So what messages did I get? Something like, "You won't get what you want, but you shouldn't leave." There's no doubt that my own hesitation and ambivalence toward marriage and starting a family were influenced by these messages.

Besides affecting my relationships, the wounds, or even the *perceived* wounds, of childhood influenced many of the choices I made in life, as they do for many people. When I got sober, I was living three thousand miles from my parents and brothers, pretty much the greatest distance I could be and still be on the same continent. I came to see this distance as having both symbolic and practical meaning. I had never had any big breaks with my family, no feuds or running resentments, but our family was complicated, each of us with our own inner struggles and outer conflicts. Of course, that could be a description of the human race, but when drugs and alcohol are part of the mix, these problems can get ratcheted up to much higher levels. I was the youngest of five boys, all of us smart, funny, and insecure. Growing up, I thought my brothers were the greatest. I thought of myself as lacking in relation to them, as they captured academic prizes and went off to Harvard and Yale and careers on Wall Street.

I couldn't imagine any of that for myself; it all seemed too grown up and complicated. I also didn't feel I could compete at these things, so I chose music. Somehow, being a musician seemed like a way to avoid the comparisons with my brothers, since none of them had chosen that career. As I look back, it's clear that they weren't nearly as concerned about competing with me as I was with them. I'm sure they would have been happy to see me succeed at anything, whether I outshone them or not. But these are the strange choices we make based on the confusion of youth and the unrecognized conditioning that happens in a family.

Most of the alcoholics and addicts I meet have pretty complicated and often messy stories to tell about their families and their childhoods. When we get sober, all of this has to be confronted in one way or another. That might just mean writing inventory about it so that you understand yourself better and can figure out how to live a happy, clean, and sober life. For many of us, though, it also means reconnecting or healing our family relationships.

This is where the guidance of the Steps, the Twelve Step literature, and a sponsor, therapist, or spiritual friend is so important. The conditioning of childhood is so deep and such a part of us that it can be difficult to sort out what is true, and what are wise and skillful ways of acting with our family, from our old feelings and behaviors. Just learning to be less reactive is a critical piece. Trying to see our family members as imperfect human beings rather than as monsters or tormentors; trying to forgive their past mistakes; trying not to take everything they say or do personally; seeing that our own behavior may have had a part in the way they treated us—all of these are part of repairing these relationships and moving forward with our family.

There isn't one answer, whether to reconcile or permanently split; how open to be and how much to protect yourself; how much you can forgive and how much you simply can't. Some wounds don't heal; some acts can't be forgiven; sometimes there's no love left. If we are seeking to recover joy, then we have to find answers to these questions, find ways of living with the past and moving into the future.

If there aren't irreconcilable wounds, many of us find that repairing or deepening nuclear family ties can be an important part of bringing more contentment and a sense of wholeness into our recovery. Even with the struggles and conflicts of growing up in a family, the ties that are created in childhood are usually the deepest we'll ever form outside of those with our own partner and children. As I've gotten older, when I have a conversation with one of my brothers, the depth of connection, the sense of shared history, worldview, and even sense of humor have surprised me. For an addict, there can be such a sense of alienation from the world, such a feeling of disconnection, that to discover—or remember—in recovery that there are people with whom you feel totally at home can be a great relief.

REFLECTION **Past Family Karma**

Begin by reflecting on the state of your family relationships. Where are the wounds and where are the positive connections? Are there relationships that have drifted apart that could be revived? Is there history that you don't feel ready to face right now?

Consider, too, how you've been shaped, for better or for worse, by your family history. It can be helpful to reflect on the good stuff you got from your family, as well as acknowledging the bad. Take some time, as well, to appreciate what your family of origin gave you. Since you are reading this book, there's something in you that wants to survive and make a better life, and that in itself owes something to your family karma. What training, talents, or skills did you gain from your family that help you today?

If there are some relationships that deserve reconsideration, make a commitment to reconnect with those people. ▪

REFLECTION **Family Karma Today**

Now reflect on how you can move forward given your past. How is your family history affecting your relationships today? Are there ways in which you are unconsciously re-creating those past relationships, or, on the other hand, creating their opposite? You may not be able to undo deep conditioning, but you can at least be more aware of it, and perhaps avoid letting it control you.

Finally, if you have children, consider how you have created karma for them, both good and bad. How has your past affected the way you raised your own children? How can you be more skillful in the way you treat them? And, lastly, seeing how difficult it is not to pass on your own negative traits, perhaps offer some forgiveness to your own parents and other family members whose imperfections may have harmed you. ▪

Family Dharma

When I got sober, I noticed that people with more time than I had seemed to be doing two things: going back to school and starting a family. While I'd had a very negative attitude about school since dropping out, it did seem possible to return. But becoming a parent—that was another story. First of all, marriage itself felt really alien to me. The combination of watching my unhappy parents, being a hippie who rejected traditional roles, becoming a musician who wanted freedom and lack of responsibility, and having an incapacity for staying with one woman made marriage seem beyond me. And yet, in just a few years of recovery, as so many of those elements of my self-image fell away, the idea of being a grown-up with grown-up relationships and grown-up responsibilities no longer seemed so onerous, and, in fact, started to have a certain appeal.

It took many years for this all to play out, for me to meet the right person and for us to be ready, but when I did get married and a year later became a father, a great deal had changed, not least my understanding of what brings happiness.

I had always thought that being "free" was the most important thing, and parenthood seemed like the opposite of freedom. I was afraid of being responsible for someone else, as I found it hard enough to be responsible for myself. I thought that my happiness depended on being able to go where I wanted and do what I wanted when I wanted.

It's remarkable how quickly all those beliefs and the fears that drove them fell away when I became a father.

If I'm going to tell you about happiness, I have to say that holding my just-born daughter in my arms was the most joyful, thrilling moment of my life. I soon realized that I had been missing out on something essential and human for a long time, that my conditioning and upbringing and personality had conspired to delude me, to create a fear that obscured this most essential human joy, the joy of parenting. In fact, before that, I'd never even liked children at all.

All of a sudden, not only was I in love with my own child, but I found myself caring for and interested in the children of my friends and all the children who started to come into my life through play dates and preschool and onward. Even today, I feel a great parental love and concern for my now-teenage daughter's friends. It is as though becoming a parent opened up the world for me. Today, when I talk to a younger person or young relative who is trying to decide whether to have a child, I tell them about my own experience and how, until you have a child, you can't grasp the feeling of love that you will have, the incomparable richness that becoming a parent will bring into your life.

When my daughter was a toddler, I helped start a family meditation group, mainly to support parents of young children who felt that parenting was taking away from their meditation practice. Many Buddhist practitioners have difficulty reconciling their commitment to a spiritual path with the life of a householder. The Buddha's story might not be the most helpful in this regard, since he left his wife and infant and went off to get enlightened. Of course, he became the Buddha, so it's hard to fault him. When he talked to monks, he kind of disparaged the householder's life, saying it was "crowded and dusty." I've never understood what he meant by "dusty," but clearly he didn't see it as ideal for meditative development.

Nonetheless, according to Bhikkhu Bodhi, the great Buddhist translator, the Buddha believed that "It is the close, loving relationship between parents and children that fosters the virtues and sense of humane responsibility essential to a cohesive social order. Within the family, these values are transmitted from one generation to the next, and thus a harmonious society is highly dependent on harmonious relations between parents and children." In typical Buddhist fashion, this takes the focus off personal wishes and puts it on more universal—or in this case, societal—issues. We think we get married and have kids to satisfy our own wants, but when we step back, we see that we are actually participating in a web of interdependence, building a "harmonious society." When viewed in this way, we can hold our family life in a more impersonal way, as part of something larger.

I've done my own exploration of the spirituality of marriage and parenting. Clearly becoming a parent opens us to an experience of love like no other. When my daughter was an infant, a Thai monk told my wife and me that "Metta is Mother Love." The Buddha himself makes this comparison in the Metta Sutta when he says, "Even as a mother protects her only child with her life, so with a boundless heart should one cherish all living beings."

At one point, I had some fun drawing parallels between monastic and married life, since some of the parents I knew were feeling that their spiritual practice was lacking in comparison to the monks they admired. Here are some of the connections I made:

- Monks ordain, making a commitment to their way of life in front of their community; parents marry, making a commitment to their way of life in front of their community. Ordination is a sacrament, a holy act; marriage is a sacrament, a holy act.

- Monks take a vow of celibacy; marriage traditionally includes a vow of fidelity. Working with sexuality as a celibate is a difficult and powerful practice; working with sexuality in a relationship is a difficult and powerful practice.

- All possessions are shared in the monastery; finances are shared in the family. Monastics have to let go of many of their material desires; parents have to let go of many of their material desires—and kids too have to learn to let go. Not acting on our wishes reveals the power and pain of desire. Acting on desires shows the unsatisfactory nature of that which we crave.

- In the monastery, decisions are made for the greater good of the community, and the individual's desires are secondary; in the family, decisions are made for the greater good of the family, and the individual's desires are secondary.

- In the monastery, you are thrown together with a group of people you might not always like, but you have to make the best of it; in the family, you are thrown together with a group of people you might not always like, but you have to make the best of it.

- In the monastery, we try to express our love in every activity; in the family, we try to express our love in every activity.

- You never graduate from the monastery; you never graduate from your family.

Is this all an exaggeration? Sure it is, but it points to the ways that we can recast our understanding of our lives. About monastic life, Ajahn Amaro says: "It's not like ordinary human life with some bits cut out. It endeavors to manifest in the physical realm our innate, divine, transcendent nature. That's why many people find monasticism both appealing and frightening." Something like this could be said of parenting: It's not like just adding in some kids and losing all the fun of being a couple. It's something completely different, a difference that can only be understood in its own context.

I made this list mainly because I think it's important to find the spirituality inherent to any situation. I think it's unfortunate to see your family life as impinging on your spiritual aspirations, and to remember that it's our approach to our lives that creates a spiritual experience, not the particular circumstances. That's not to say that there aren't some circumstances that make it very difficult to find a spiritual essence, but certainly family life has great potential for opening us to deep wisdom and love.

REFLECTION **Stress and Intention in Family Life**

One of our biggest family problems is stress. Many of us feel overextended, overworked, and burnt out. What to do?

First, we go back to intention and look at our priorities in light of it. What's really important? What can be dropped?

Then, before we make a commitment to do something, we check whether the stress it will bring is worth the payoff. ▪

PRACTICE **A Balanced Family Life**

Once you've reflected on stress in your family life, consider these changes:

Simplify. Read more, watch less—the TV, computer, and other screens drain us. Drive less, walk/bike more—the car is very stressful. What are you doing just out of habit or the sense that you're "supposed" to? Can you drop some of your activities? How about an "at-home vacation"—a couple days off without going anywhere?

Meditate. Find times to fit in daily practice: sit before the kids get up; at work, close the door of your office for ten or twenty minutes or go to your car in the parking lot and sit; take a mindful walk; practice after the kids go to sleep or ask your partner to give you a meditation break—to watch the kids or take them for a walk while you practice.

Be mindful. Mindfulness isn't just for meditation. Pay attention to the little moments and activities. Be present and enjoy.

Balance caring for others and caring for yourself. The kids won't be happy if we're not happy; at the same time, we won't be happy if the kids aren't happy. Sometimes they really need us, and sometimes they are just being demanding. Try to discern the difference. Sometimes we just have to stop, breathe, and give them a hug or rub their back. Bring them back into their bodies, even as you bring yourself back into your own body.

Remember impermanence. Above all, remember that this little (or big) family is only here for a moment. Soon it will be gone—the kids will be grown and have left the house, and you will be old and looking back on these brief years. Don't squander them, don't fight them; embrace them as best you can. Every day there is beauty, every day there is the call for your presence, for your awakening; don't turn away. ▪

Gurus, Sponsors, and Shrinks

Among the most important relationships we have in our lives are those with our teachers, mentors, sponsors, and therapists. Even the Buddha had teachers who were important on his path. In various Buddhist traditions, the teacher holds different levels of importance. In the Twelve Step world, the role of a sponsor can be critical. And many of us find that we need professional therapeutic help at some point in our lives as well. All of these relationships have positive and negative potential. Because they are relationships that involve power, they are very delicate, and it's important that, even though we might be the student, sponsee, or patient/client—in other words, the person with less power in the relationship—we take responsibility for our role in this relationship.

Clearly, every one of us is going to need help in our lives, especially if we are dealing with addiction. My own sponsor showed me much more than how to work the Steps. I had no success trying to meditate until I started to work with teachers. And the insights and attitudes I've gotten from various therapists have been an important part of my personal growth. So we need these people—at least I do.

I've found navigating these relationships to be complicated. The biggest difficulty is that because they are the experts, I am somewhat in the dark as to whether they are steering me in the right direction or not. It's only now after decades of work with such people that I have enough confidence to feel like an equal in these relationships.

While I am trying to focus on the positive in this book, I am going to start, at least, by looking at the risks in these relationships and see if I can draw some positive lessons.

Therapists

My family was typical of a certain class of people in the 1950s who went to psychiatrists like someone goes to yoga class today. Cocktail parties, golf at the country club, and appointments with the shrink. My father was a lawyer so we were comfortable financially—though he wasn't ambitious, so we weren't rich. Nonetheless, all my brothers and my mother, but not my father, saw a therapist. In fact, many of them saw the same psychiatrist, which probably couldn't even happen today.

As the youngest in the family, I always assumed that my time would come, and it did, when I was fourteen. That's when I began to experience depression, and my parents packed me off to a different doctor. I would go and sit with him once a week and talk. He was quite a storyteller and did a lot of the talking himself. I had no idea how any of this was supposed to help, but I had a blind faith that psychiatry had some kind of magic that would kick in at some point.

It never did.

Over the next five years, I would go through a string of psychiatrists and psychologists before swearing off the whole profession for fifteen years.

What went wrong in those relationships? Clearly, I was troubled and confused, and certainly rebellious. None of this helped. But I think the approach to treatment in psychiatry and therapy at the time also had a hand in the problems. I think that a therapist should be able to explain in some coherent way how they view the process of healing and change that they hope to facilitate. At the time, it was all smoke and mirrors—at least to me it was. Maybe they had a plan, some idea about how they were going to help me, but I'll never know.

I suppose one of the central questions for me with any psycho-spiritual system has been "How does this work?" That's why I like Theravadan Buddhism, as least as it's been brought to the West. It's very clear about a process. The Twelve Steps are also pretty clear, although I think some of their process gets unnecessarily mystified.

When I came back to therapy in Los Angeles at age thirty-four, just a year before I got sober, I didn't have the same expectations I did as a teenager. I was skeptical, but also grateful to have someone intelligent to talk to. I felt as if unraveling some of my past, my upbringing and my relationships with my parents and brothers, was important, and I think it was. It didn't solve anything, but it started to give me some basis for understanding myself. And it can't be a coincidence that I got sober soon after that, although there was no direct relationship—that is, the therapist didn't encourage me to stop drinking and using, presumably because I didn't focus on that issue in therapy. (I think I'm typical in that way. Many alcoholics/addicts don't see their use of drugs and alcohol as their main problem, at least not until they get clean and sober.)

I've continued off and on to see therapists over the years, but now my approach is completely different. First of all, I'm mostly interested in a cognitive-behavioral approach that blends with my mindfulness practice and focuses on thoughts, feelings, and behaviors in the present. Unraveling past causes isn't that interesting to me or particularly useful. Rather, I want to look at my limiting and negative beliefs, my reactivity, and what kinds of helpful behaviors and views I can adopt to deal with these issues. The point is that I am interested in practical solutions. The Buddha says that trying to unravel past causes is a fruitless and frustrating task, and that seems to apply to therapy as well.

What's especially different is that my relationship with therapists seems more collaborative now, not hierarchical or patriarchal. I don't know if without my life experience this would still be possible, but I do think that openness about the process on the part of the therapist is important.

Finally, I think the hardest thing for me in dealing with therapists goes back to my original issue: I want them to fix me. I've come to see that it's my own engagement in a process, my own actions, both inner and outer, that is the key to my mental health and happiness. A therapist can help me to see what I need to do in that process and perhaps to understand how some of the feelings arise, but I have to do the work. For an addict who was always looking for an external and automatic answer to my problems, this will probably always be a frustrating fact to accept.

REFLECTION **Therapists**

Take some time to consider the relationships you may have had
with therapists. What did you expect from them? What did you
get? Have you been realistic in this regard? Were you clear about
what you wanted from them? ■

Gurus

When The Beatles went to India in the sixties with Maharishi Mahesh Yogi to study Transcendental Meditation (TM), many of us were exposed for the first time to the idea of a guru, a wise, enlightened being who could help us to transform in some way. As with the therapists of the time, gurus were shrouded in mystery and magic. I dreamed of having a relationship with someone like this, someone who would intuitively know what I needed and would give it to me through some mystical process. It sounds like I was looking for a fairy godmother, or maybe just an *actual* mother. I probably was.

When I learned TM it wasn't from a guru, but just someone who'd been trained to teach this fairly simple practice. I was a little disappointed that I wasn't meeting some Indian sage, but I also felt more comfortable working with someone like me, a young American. Two years later, when I started practicing Buddhist meditation, my first teacher was an American monk who had just returned from several years in Sri Lanka. This was more like it. Only, beneath his robes, he was just another guy, and something of an eccentric and controlling guy at that. I fell into what for me became a typical pattern with teachers, first idolizing him and later rejecting him.

It's not surprising that we act out old patterns in our relationships with our teachers. I wanted to be rescued, and maybe parented, by my teachers, but at first I didn't find anyone willing to take on that role. Soon after meeting this monk, I went on retreat with Jack Kornfield and Joseph Goldstein, two of the leading Western Buddhist meditation teachers. As inspiring as they were, they didn't play the guru game, and they had good boundaries. I learned a lot from them, but something in me still wanted more. That's when I met "Ananda."

I'd spent a year working with Jack and Joseph, taking a three-week and then a three-month retreat with them and other teachers. These were powerful and transforming experiences, but in some sense, not yet being sober, I wasn't ready to be transformed. Ananda, as this average-looking American I met one day in Boston called himself, offered the magic I sought. Through a confusing, eclectic mix of practices, rituals, and beliefs, he claimed that he could help me get enlightened quickly.

Leaving my job, my friends, the band I'd just joined, and all my belongings, I set out on a road trip to "live on faith" with him. This was a radical step, a desperate grasping for something that drove me toward what would eventually be my bottom. Only two months into our travels, I gave up on Ananda's path. Homeless now, I lived on the streets of Venice Beach for months, relying on the help of friends and a couple of low-brow gigs with my guitar. The dream was over. It started to dawn on me that I was reaching too high, and being in such desperate straits made me appreciate the simplest of things: a meal, a bed, a job. I started to rebuild my life, chastened by my experiences, and finally got things together enough to see that I had a problem with drugs and alcohol. It's clear now that the same thing that drove me to find a guru and a mystical spiritual fix for my life also drove my drinking and using. Both were attempts to deal with life without actually facing reality.

We need teachers—I needed teachers. But we have to be careful what we expect from them. Not only can I put unreasonable expectations on my teachers, but some teachers also take advantage of vulnerable students. The power that we give to spiritual authority can go to the teacher's head—or some other part of their body. The sex and money scandals that have torn apart many spiritual communities are a result of these two things: the flawed teacher exploiting his power and the flawed community idealizing and enabling the teacher. When we give someone too much power because we want them to take care of us, to fix us, we are opening the door for abuse.

Developing a healthy relationship with a skillful teacher is challenging. This is compounded by the realities of the lives of teachers today. Many have to travel extensively and teach hundreds or even thousands of people each year. It's going to be difficult for them to take time to work with people individually on an ongoing or long-term basis.

If you are looking for a teacher, these are some of the questions you need to ask: First, what is it that I want, and is that a realistic or healthy thing to seek from a teacher? Next, what can they give—are they available to work with me? And finally, what am I willing to do as a student? Am I willing to take guidance or do I just want someone to tell me that I'm okay?

Today I talk about many people as my teachers, some of whom I've barely met. Even reading someone's book can make you feel like their student. Most of the time, I realize that I don't need personal guidance because what the teacher is suggesting is right there in her talks or writings. If I consider what I've heard her say and write and apply it to my life and my practice, it becomes pretty clear what guidance I would get if I asked.

Ultimately, we are our own teachers. There's no one who can get inside our heads or walk around with us all day. We are with ourselves twenty-four hours a day; we can see our own thoughts, words, and actions; we can learn to guide ourselves if we pay careful attention.

REFLECTION **Teachers**

Take some time to consider the relationships you may have had with spiritual teachers. What did you expect from them? What did you get? Have you been realistic in this regard? Were you clear about what you wanted from them?

If you are seeking a teacher, consider what you are really seeking from that relationship. Are these realistic expectations? ■

Sponsors

The formal role of a sponsor in Twelve Step programs is to guide you through the Steps. That's important, and in my own work, I certainly wasn't ready to approach Step Four, the "searching and fearless moral inventory," without a sponsor. Many sponsors, including mine, do much more than this, acting as a kind of life coach for addicts who often have few basic life skills. My sponsor helped me to find common-sense solutions to problems that had once stymied me. He often just gave me a "one day at a time" approach, suggesting that I do what I could today and not get overwhelmed by the size of my problems or the time it might take to finish a task. That advice has served me well, especially in the task of writing books.

A sponsor is someone who not only helps us to navigate the Steps, but also the program itself. Since Twelve Step programs have no official leaders or authorities, when you come into a meeting, you might hear a lot of conflicting opinions, some of which might be uninformed, to say the least. Since anyone can share, and no one is supposed to interrupt or argue with anyone, all kinds of ideas can get tossed out. This is quite different from the very hierarchical structure of Buddhist communities that are built around the wisdom of the teachers.

So a good sponsor is a trustworthy guide and support, especially as you navigate early recovery. Unfortunately, not every sponsor is a skillful one.

There is no training to be a sponsor, no diploma or authorization. Essentially, sponsorship is simply the formal work of Step Twelve, "to carry the message" to another addict. There are as many approaches to the Steps as there are members of the program, so each sponsor will have their own approach. I'm sure most do a good job, but naturally enough, there are plenty who don't.

For someone with a nontraditional religious or nonreligious orientation, this is where things can get problematic. My sponsor never questioned my Buddhist orientation, and what I inferred from his approach is that it's not the sponsor's job to tell you what your Higher Power should be. Unfortunately, this isn't always the case. Because I teach a nontraditional approach to the Steps, I've been privy to quite a few stories of sponsors who found Buddhism to be an unacceptable path for working the Twelve Steps.

Since the Steps explicitly say that we can work with "God, *as we understood him,*" it's clearly a violation of that principle for a sponsor, or anyone else, to tell you how to believe. Further, the implication of "as we understood him" is that we should be following our own spiritual path, not one set down by a sponsor or anyone else. The point is that we need a concept of God or Higher Power that helps us to work the Steps and get the benefits they offer. The Twelve Step community is a place where we are supposed to put aside our personal opinions about politics, religion, or anything else, and simply support each other in our work to recover and lead happy and productive lives.

Another big problem for people in working with a sponsor is the common trait of rebelliousness and resistance to authority that many addicts have. Anyone who turns to addictive behaviors as a way of life is clearly rebelling against society's boundaries, and so it's not surprising that many of us rebel against anyone's suggestions or guidance. In early recovery, we might even be encouraged to "take the cotton out of our ears and put it in our mouths," a classic Twelve Step cliché that actually captures something important.

Most of us addicts have screwed up our lives pretty badly by the time we come into a program. We have developed beliefs about ourselves, the world, and life that are incredibly unproductive, and very often completely misguided. There is a certain view in Twelve Step programs of newcomers being like hopeless, helpless children, and that's often enough true. Sponsors are often skeptical of the decision-making skills of newcomers, and therefore may be derisive of their plans or life strategies. For the person who has truly hit bottom in their addiction and in their life, surrender to the guidance of a clear-eyed and experienced sponsor may come as a relief, and such a surrender can be a valuable first step in putting a life back together.

However, there are risks in this kind of dominance by an untrained nonprofessional (indeed, there are risks even from a trained professional). Not every newcomer needs this kind of overarching control, and if, as is sometimes the case, this is a sponsor's unvarying strategy, the newcomer might be driven away from what they perceive as an infantilizing and disrespectful process. Not all addicts are so desperate or misguided.

In some recovery communities, the control goes even further, down to how people dress or wear their hair, and here I think a line has been crossed. It's certainly true that for a certain type of alcoholic or addict who never learned even the basics of grooming and cleanliness, there's sometimes a need for intervention on this level. People who became hope-to-die junkies as teenagers, never held a job, and never dealt with any of the ordinary challenges and responsibilities of adulthood are going to need a lot of hand-holding. But to apply this type of sponsorship to everyone risks losing a lot of people who simply don't need that much help.

This brings us to my fundamental belief about sponsorship: I don't think one-size-fits-all is the way to go. While there can be a great temptation to simply give a standard set of instructions to every person you sponsor, this is simply not very effective. This brings up another philosophical principle: some people think that all addicts and alcoholics are alike, and therefore should be treated the same way. In fact, this idea is a response to what's called "terminal uniqueness," the habit of addicts to think that their situation is different, that no one understands them, and that no standardized program could help them. This sense of being special and different is a fairly common characteristic of people who need, but haven't found, recovery, and I've often addressed it with people I've been trying to help. But this idea of fitting every addict into a box is, I think, an overreaction to this tendency.

What I try to do when I talk with a newcomer is keep two things in mind: the signs of typical addict thinking and behavior, and the more unique elements of the person's story and makeup that need to be respected. I've found that if I just dismiss someone as "another addict," they feel disrespected and not understood. This simply alienates them. And, although I often detect a lot of typical elements in their story, if they feel they are being heard, they are more likely to respond to whatever direction I give them. The fact is, one unskillful word from a sponsor or person experienced in recovery can turn off a newcomer and trigger relapse. This isn't to say that the sponsor is responsible for the relapse; only that these are potentially volatile relationships that must be approached with care, wisdom, and compassion.

Although I began this section in talking about how one deals with a sponsor, I've wound up talking also about how to *be* a sponsor. Many people find that as they are in recovery and their lives progress, they will grow into new roles—as sponsors, as therapists, or as teachers. In fact, it is through our own struggles that we develop the skills to move into these roles. Every spiritual tradition encourages us to be of service, and as we mature in our recovery, many opportunities will arise. It's so important that we take care in how we move into these roles, that we watch the arising of ego, ambition, and self-promotion that can distort and undermine our pull to service. The role of guide and helper carries great power and responsibility. We need to always remember our original impulse, draw from our own experience, and maintain great humility in the face of human suffering over which, ultimately, we have so little control.

REFLECTION **Sponsors**

Take some time to consider the relationships you may have had with sponsors. What did you expect from them? What did you get? Have you been realistic in this regard? Were you clear about what you wanted from them? ■

4

FORTY HOURS OF HAPPINESS

finding joy in work

Finding meaningful and satisfying work is one of the great tasks of growing up. Balancing that work with the rest of our lives is another great task. Our sense of self-worth, our place in the world, and our sense of wholeness are strongly supported by a rich work life, whether in the marketplace or at home.

Following Your Bliss

It's commonly said that the two big issues of life in recovery are finance and romance, and this was certainly the case for me. I've told you about my struggles to achieve a stable relationship. At the same time that I was working on those issues, I was trying to figure out what my career would be post-music.

Although I never made much money or had much worldly success as a musician, I consider myself very lucky to have spent so many years playing music for a living. People often tell me that they envy my experience as a professional musician. I was very fortunate to find something I loved, and I worked hard at it. Once I started in as a full-time musician, my days would involve my own practicing and song writing, band rehearsals, and the gigs themselves. Often I played six nights a week, and traveled for months at a time from one hotel to another. It wasn't until I finally stopped living this way that I realized how hard I'd been working all those years. I always thought I was getting away with something by not having a day job. And, in a sense, I was. I certainly wasn't working at a tedious, unfulfilling job. I was doing something I loved, even with all the caveats, like playing Top 40 songs in Holiday Inn lounges. So, in the sense of having what for me was meaningful work, I was doing well. But, in most other senses, I wasn't.

My choice to become a musician was in a way at the opposite end of the scale from someone who pursues a career in a field they don't care about just to make money. I suspect that choice is more common than mine. Many people either don't have a passion or are afraid to pursue their passion for fear of failure and poverty. This is not an easy problem to solve, but I think that finding a balance between doing something we love and making a comfortable living is important to finding happiness.

For addicts, this problem is compounded by the fact that all we really want to do is get loaded. Nonetheless, I've met lots of addicts who were successful professionally even as they worked their way to an alcoholic or drug-addicted bottom. The compulsivity and obsessiveness of addicts sometimes spills over into their work life. In fact, an addictive energy is often what drives very successful people, which is why we see so many famous people succumbing to addiction. Craving, insecurity, obsession, and the desire to control can lead both ways: to worldly success and to addictive self-destruction.

A year into my recovery, I finally got off the road. At that point, I found a job as a messenger in LA and started to form my own band. I wanted to stay in the area, and the band I had been with wanted to travel. I had no idea, really, how I was going to move forward in making a living or having a career, whether I was going to remain a professional musician or if some other option might arise, but now that I was fully committed to recovery and to the Twelve Steps, I had some faith that things would work out.

One of the first ideas I had was that I would go into the business side of music, maybe as a producer or working at a record company. One day, I mentioned this idea in a Twelve Step meeting, and afterward someone approached me to tell me that his cousin worked for a record company and he would introduce me. This was the kind of help that I was finding so often in meetings as I "turned my will and my life over."

I called his cousin, and soon had an internship at an independent label. A year working on the inside, the other side from where I'd always been, made it clear that this wasn't my path. I couldn't stand the way the record company treated their artists, withholding royalties and cutting corners. I was amazed that people in a record company didn't know the difference between a Les Paul and a Stratocaster. I realized that they weren't really in the music business—just the money business.

I was trying to follow the clues to finding a stable job, if not a career, and one thing I discovered while working at the record company was that the ability to type was valued in the workplace. So, while my fantasy of discovering the next great band was gone, I settled for something a little more modest, taking typing and computer classes at the occupational training school down the street from the house I was sharing in Venice Beach. Oddly enough, I found that I really liked typing. It felt like playing an instrument. And learning my way around a computer was fascinating. This was 1988, and I'd had very little exposure to PCs. Next thing I knew, the Santa Monica-Malibu Unified School District needed some temporary data-entry help, and I got the job.

One of the key principles of recovery is acceptance. Step Three points toward this, and the AA Big Book contains a famous passage that begins, "Acceptance is the answer to all my problems today." Acceptance is the antidote to the tendency of addicts to be overly controlling, to resist change, and to demand that life follow their script. My own unwillingness to give up my meager existence as a musician was typical of this kind of resistance. It reflected an extremely narrow view of my life's possibilities and a refusal to explore experiences and careers that were outside my comfort zone.

Now, at almost three years sober and thirty-eight years old, I was finally open to change. I came into this temp job with humility and willingness—and not a little desperation. This was the first time I'd ever worked full-time in an office, something that in my narrow thinking I had not only feared, but disparaged. I found that it wasn't so bad. In fact, the work engaged my mind, the setting was comfortable, and the boss and other workers were pleasant.

During the course of the month-long contract, I had to go to the personnel office several times. I hit it off with the women there, and when the data-entry job ended, they offered me a position in their office. As I settled into this more secure job, I started to see more clearly why someone would want to work like this. My life as a musician was extremely insecure, having to constantly be looking for new gigs, playing with unreliable musicians, sometimes getting fired or not even paid. Now all I had to do was show up and put in my hours, and I not only was sure to get a check each week, but I also got medical and retirement benefits as well as sick leave and vacation. Such things had been inconceivable when I was playing bars. I quickly took advantage of my dental plan and got some cavities filled.

Silly as it sounds, one of the first things that had motivated me to be a musician had been the fact that I wouldn't have to get up in the morning. Even that had ceased to be a problem now that I wasn't getting drunk and stoned every night. The whole shift into normality felt like a great relief, much like getting sober itself. I was discovering the simple pleasure of work.

As an addict, I'd thought that work had to be glorious, romantic, and inspiring, and that's what I thought I would get from music. I never got that—well, yes, there were thrilling moments, but they certainly weren't the norm—but I still clung to that dream. Letting go of that dream was allowing me to see what life and happiness were really about.

The willingness that brought me to that job was becoming a key part of my life. What became evident was that if taking a little class on typing and computers could be so enjoyable and have such a positive effect on my life, going back to school on a more serious level could open even more doors.

That summer, I walked onto the campus of Santa Monica College and enrolled. Twenty years after my last attempts at high school, I was starting again. That walk across the lawn in front of the administration building is still clear in my memory as I recited the Serenity Prayer over and over to give myself the courage to walk through those doors. The true adventure of my life began that day.

REFLECTION **My Work**

Take some time to reflect on your own work life. Is it satisfying? Is it meaningful for you? If you are doing the same work you did before recovery, consider what your original impulses were to enter that line of work and whether they still apply today. Ask yourself if you are doing what you are doing out of fear of change or failure, or because you really want to do it.

We can't all be inspired and passionate about our profession, so another question is, What are you making of the work you have? Even if it's not your passion, do you bring mindfulness and care to your work? Do you treat your colleagues with kindness and compassion?

Finally, if you aren't doing work that you love, what would it take to change? Would it be possible to find work that really engaged you? Maybe you don't have to know exactly how to get there, but can you think of what the first step might be to moving toward something more meaningful? Today, many people change professions several times in their work life. I wouldn't say, "It's never too late," but I do believe that if we are still interested and healthy enough to work, we can pursue many possibilities. ▪

Creativity and Work

I often hear people who don't work in the arts say something like, "I'm not a creative person." This always strikes me as a very limited viewpoint. Humans are inherently creative. One doesn't have to be playing music, writing poetry, or making paintings to express creativity. I've seen creative computer programmers and creative department managers. If we engage in our work, we'll naturally be creative. Just seeing this can be inspiring. So, I think it's important that we broaden our definition of creativity to include any activity that engages us, so we can take more joy in our work and play.

Creativity is one of the most joyful of human acts. When we apply imagination, problem-solving, and present-moment engagement to a task, there are several positive outcomes. First is the immediate pleasure we get from being absorbed in an activity. Undistracted activity brings the joy of concentration, one of the forms of joy the Buddha identified. This joy derives from dropping worries about the future or regrets about the past. In this state of focus, the body is relaxed and alert, the mind open and receptive. Entering this state of absorption brings a heightened state of aliveness and sense of connection to ourselves, to others, and to the world around us.

Another pleasure that comes from creativity is the pleasure of making something, accomplishing something, or solving something. When we complete a task successfully, there is a sense of pride and accomplishment in seeing what we've done. Each of us wants to have an impact on the world, and seeing the results of our work gives the immediate sense that we've added something that wasn't there before.

This pride then leads to a third form of joy in creativity: the sense of self-worth that comes in seeing that we are capable and creative, in knowing that we can bring something positive to the world.

Mindfulness is the vital component in the development of these forms of joy. It is the essential element of creativity, that which allows us to engage fully in an activity to begin with. As we deepen this capacity of engagement, our mind becomes more supple and starts to naturally incline toward a present-moment connection where creativity flows more easily. This intuitive experience becomes something we can access at will, a natural part of our daily life.

Mindfulness also helps us to see the different forms of joy that stem from creative action. If we aren't paying attention, we won't see or appreciate that which flows from our creative state. Joy comes when we are aware of the goodness in our lives, and that awareness depends on mindfulness. This may seem obvious, but the truth is, we often miss the joy and pleasure that are right in front of us because our attention is distracted. Creativity, like all activities, is only appreciated when we take joy in it.

It's unfortunate that in our culture, creativity is often associated with addiction. We see so many examples of musicians, actors, and writers who are alcoholics or addicts. This has created a false impression that somehow drugs and alcohol help creativity. I've even heard of jazz musicians who believed they needed to be junkies if they wanted to play like Charlie Parker. I've also known recovering artists who struggled for a time to get the flow of creativity back when they quit drinking and using. While I used to depend on marijuana to fuel my songwriting sessions, I don't believe that creativity is actually tied to drugs or alcohol, despite the correlations.

Artists become addicts for the same reasons everyone else does. Certainly for me, the musician lifestyle made acting on my addictions easy. But listening to the music I wrote and performed in those days easily refutes the idea that I was more creative when loaded. Often my songs lacked polish and reflected a laziness in my efforts. When you're stoned, everything sounds good, so the critical faculty, so important in evaluating and refining creative works, is dulled, allowing you to accept substandard work as complete. Yes, for some people mild intoxication can help them to suppress the stifling effects of self-criticism that sometimes block artists' expressive capacity, but meditation can do the same thing in a much more healthy, conscious, and repeatable way.

I think it's a mistake to look at creativity as a side issue or hobby to pursue. Creativity has special qualities that make it one of the most important healing activities in recovery. The self-inflicted wounds and hatred that we carry need real care. It's not always enough to work the Steps and meditate a lot. The proactive behavior of creativity gives us something real to look at, something that shows our worth in the world. It can start to replace our bad memories and broken lives with something positive and forward pointing. As addicts, we desperately need positive input, a positive self-image, and uplifting feelings and experiences. We need to engage life in a constructive way, and bringing this quality of creativity into all our activities, from the most mundane tasks to the most profound, is one vital way to do this.

REFLECTION   **Bringing Creativity to Life**

Start by looking at how you are already creative in your life. Then ask yourself how you could bring more creativity. Remember that creativity is an attitude, so begin by looking at how you can bring more of that attitude into the things you are already doing. Then think about other activities you could engage in that would allow this precious quality to manifest more in your life. ■

Workaholism

Overworking has many negative effects on our happiness: The stress impacts our health. We don't have enough spare time to be with friends and family, much less support groups like Twelve Step meetings and those in the spiritual community. Exercise and inner work are often abandoned. And we are left on an island of work with nothing left to support our happiness and mental health. Eventually, such a situation collapses, perhaps from deteriorating health, relapse, emotional over-whelm, loneliness, or some combination of all these factors. As one teacher puts it, "It's hard to imagine that on your deathbed you will think, 'I wish I'd spent more time at the office.'"

At four years sober, I found myself caught in an overwork spiral. In June of 1989, Santa Monica College had a writers' conference. I'd been enrolled in a creative-writing course that spring semester and my teacher suggested I attend. He liked a short story I'd written about a band on the road based on some experiences I'd had. The highlight of the conference for me was meeting with a writer I greatly admired, Kem Nunn, and having him comment on my story. His main sugges-tion: write a novel about this character.

At this point in my recovery, I was learning to follow direction from trusted people. I would never have had the courage to try to write a novel, much less the confidence that I could do it, if Kem hadn't told me to. So, I set out to write *Ghosttown*.

By that summer, I was enrolled full-time in community college, was working full-time in the Santa Monica-Malibu Unified School District personnel office, was still playing gigs with my band on most weekends, and managed to attend about five or six Twelve Step meetings every week. And, by the way, I was writing a novel.

At the end of the summer, my girlfriend broke up with me. Her reason: I wasn't giving her any time. She had a very good point.

Looking back, it's hard for me to conceive how I got all that done. But I do know that I felt a sense of urgency and excitement in my life, and I wanted to do it all. These feelings came from a couple sources. One was the fact that I had energy and clarity now that I hadn't had over the decades of addiction. Marijuana and alcohol had drained me psychically, physically, and emotionally, and now I was bouncing back. Another, perhaps more important source of these feelings was the sense that I had to catch up. Here I was in my late thirties trying to get a college degree and build some kind of security in my life. And I still had a tremendous creative impulse that had started to shift focus from music to creative writing.

It may have been a great gift that I had this energy and drive, but, as my girlfriend's decision pointed out, it was unsustainable.

I think many people in recovery wind up in similar situations. I've often heard people say that they relapsed because all the benefits of recovery wound up distracting them from the recovery itself. They became so "successful" and so busy that they had no time for meetings or other recovery work, and somehow thought that just working hard and fulfilling their responsibilities was more important than getting to a meeting or meditating or connecting with a friend or sponsor or teacher.

The Big Book has a response to this when it says that our sobriety is "contingent upon the daily maintenance of our spiritual condition."

Oddly enough, I've seen the same thing happen to Buddhist teachers. During my own teacher training, after a year or so, a large segment of the cohort started to talk about how they were getting overwhelmed with teaching responsibilities. As new teachers, many of us didn't want to turn down any opportunities, and also felt a responsibility to help anyone who asked us. Pretty soon, many of us realized we were falling into the same kind of patterns as those in the larger population. But we were supposed to be more conscious about these things, to understand the need for self-care. It only goes to show that no one is immune to these pressures and impulses.

We live in a culture that's particularly demanding. In many companies, there's a culture of workaholism, and the person who wants to follow a standard work schedule may be considered uncommitted and perhaps disloyal. In this context, it can be difficult to determine what a healthy balance between work and personal life even looks like, much less be able to implement it. Furthermore, economic pressures make it necessary for many people to work more than they'd like. And finally, the growth of technological interconnectedness has allowed work to filter into every moment of our lives, so that the traditional division between work life and personal life has broken down.

For addicts, this presents a couple of dangers. One I've already mentioned—it's the likelihood that as work takes up more and more time, self-care decreases and the potential for relapse increases. Both Buddhism and Twelve Step programs encourage routines that build in time for reflection and community support on a daily basis. Daily meditation, regular meetings, and strong relationships with a sponsor or other recovering friends help us to keep foremost in our minds those attitudes and behaviors that actually allow us to function effectively in the world. After all, while many of us may have worked at our jobs while under the influence, few of us would claim that we did our jobs better when we were loaded.

Many of us suffer from a sense of inadequacy and try to compensate by overworking. One friend talks about his sense of always being behind, never doing enough. As his company has downsized, he says that there are real facts to support this feeling because everyone in the company is expected to work more as the staff shrinks. But that reality only strengthens his already-existing sense of insecurity. And that insecurity can build into a workaholic addiction. In that case, though we may not relapse on drugs and alcohol, we may still find that excessive involvement with work undermines our emotional sobriety and, as I discovered, impacts our personal relationships in negative ways.

The truth is that sobriety, living clean, and following a spiritual path are, in many ways, counter to the dominant culture, which focuses on material gain and sensual pleasure. If we are going to live in this way, we are going to have to make some difficult choices. One well-known meditation teacher talks about walking away from his high-powered publishing career to pursue a more spiritual life. Mainstream society might view this as professional suicide, but the way he talks about it, his life of ambition and striving was the real death.

No one ever said that a spiritual life would be easy.

But for an addict, what real choice do you have?

REFLECTION   **A Balanced Work Life**

Take some time to reflect on the balance of work, home life, play, and spiritual practice in your life. Does your commitment to work allow time for these other aspects of your life? Does work stress impact your health and happiness? What changes could you make so that there would be more balance in your life? Could you maintain your economic well-being with a less intrusive work life? ∎

IT'S AN INSIDE JOB

living a mindful life

Much of what I've talked about in this book so far has seemed to be about our outer life—our behaviors, relationships, and work. All of these, however, are informed by our inner life. Until we find harmony within, we'll never find it without. Cultivating and maintaining a balanced, awakened heart and mind is the foundation of all happiness.

Meditation and Addiction

I was a teenager in the sixties and swayed by many of the new ideas that came out of that turbulent decade. When The Beatles very publicly started to practice Transcendental Meditation, it was one of those bell-ringing moments. "What is meditation?" I wondered. "Will it heal this persistent emotional turmoil? Will it put me in contact with some higher realm? Will it get me high?" I hoped it would do all these things.

I wasn't focused, disciplined, organized, or committed enough to actually pursue this nascent interest. It wasn't until the lead singer in a band I was in said he too wanted to learn to meditate—ten years after I first heard about TM—that I finally followed through.

One of the rules for learning TM is that you can't smoke marijuana for two weeks before the training. That alone was a serious impediment. At that point, it had been nine years since I'd intentionally gone a day without getting stoned. I did manage to stop smoking pot for a little while, though soon after starting to meditate, I took it up again on a semiregular basis.

As I practiced TM daily, I was disappointed in the results. My TM teacher talked about her own states of calm and bliss, but all that happened to me was that I spaced out for twenty minutes, barely remembering to repeat my mantra a dozen times. But she told me that was okay; that what was important was to just stick to it. Today, I still consider that some of the best advice I was ever given, and it's something I regularly pass on to others who are learning any form of meditation.

Years later, I would realize that my continued use of marijuana, as well as binge drinking, undermined any of the positive effects of TM. But after two years of practice and frustration, I was ready to blame TM for my lack of progress. I'd been introduced to Buddhism then, so I dropped my mantra and picked up my breath.

I threw myself into the deep end with Buddhist meditation, spending a total of four months on silent retreat in my first year of practice. But even this didn't solve all my problems, which was the deluded expectation I still had. And in the next couple years, my Buddhist practice slacked off as well.

When I finally got sober, I had been practicing meditation regularly, for better or worse, for seven years. You can interpret the fact that I was able to have a regular meditation practice while still smoking lots of pot, drinking heavily, and doing various other drugs in different ways. You could say that meditation alone wasn't enough to get me sober, and that's clearly true. But you could also say that my pursuit of a spiritual path gradually laid the groundwork for my recovery. I think that is also true. The thing is, like many addicts, I had to try a lot of different things before I figured out that drinking and using were at the root of all my problems. I've discovered that many people explore religion and spirituality before they get sober; this fits with the idea that, in their addiction, addicts are pursuing a transcendent experience, however misguided. Then again, spirituality isn't the only answer to suffering that addicts seek. Some pursue money; others pursue power or fame. Some pursue love and acceptance; others pursue thrills or danger. For an addict, none of these will satisfy us. It is only when we face the core truth that our addictive behavior, whether with substances, relationships, sex, or behaviors like gambling or spending, is the cause of our suffering that we will find our answer.

Nonetheless, part of that answer *is* meditation and a spiritual life. When practiced in the context of recovery, rather than as a fix or escape, Buddhist meditation practices can have a powerful healing and sustaining effect. Meditation brings relief from stress and anxiety; it creates energy; it leads to personal and universal insight; it brings a sense of connection to others and to the world; it offers experiences of peace and transcendence beyond anything in ordinary consciousness; it opens us to unconditional love and reveals the untapped potential of human consciousness. It brings the deepest, most profound joy.

Meditation and the Twelve Steps

Once I got sober, I was delighted to find that the Twelve Steps included meditation. Though my practice had floundered somewhat, I still "sat"—as Buddhists call seated meditation—regularly, and though I knew that meditation wasn't going to solve my addiction problem, it was important to me to continue to sit each day. It certainly helped me to weather the difficult early weeks and months of sobriety, giving me a refuge and a sense of calm in the swirl of change.

Soon, I was struck by how few of the others in recovery around me were meditating. I realized that my experience with Buddhism was somewhat unique in the Twelve Step world where the prayer part of Step Eleven seemed to be much more emphasized. When people talked about getting down on their knees in the morning, I thought, "Well, my knees are touching the floor when I meditate, even if I'm not exactly kneeling." I knew I was lucky to have my practice, and soon I began to talk about it with friends in the program. People were often interested to hear about my experience, and when I was about three years sober I started a meeting with a group of friends in which we meditated for twenty minutes at the beginning of each meeting. At the meditation meetings I'd been to before, sometimes called "Eleventh Step Meetings," we never sat for more than five minutes, so my group was certainly stretching things.

When I finally did fully re-engage with Buddhist practice around six years into my recovery, it flowed out of a more natural growth, similar to the way the Buddha suggested. His teachings to laypeople don't start with meditation instructions, but rather with guidance on morality and lifestyle. He knew that meditation was going to be much more productive if we were living in a skillful way, with morality, lovingkindness, and generosity as the foundations of our lives. When our lifestyle is based on finding immediate pleasure and gratification, very often with no concern for the welfare of others or our own long-term growth, meditation can be of only so much value. Yes, we may have some pleasant experiences, but we won't bring mindfulness into our lives in any meaningful way, because to do so would force us to look honestly at the way we are living, and that's just what we're trying to avoid doing.

My Buddhist practice started to merge with my Twelve Step program in a powerful, synergistic way. While previously I had seen the Buddhist teachings as separate from my Twelve Step program, now I began a process of integration. Twelve Step work, particularly the inventory and amends process, helps us to look at the underlying impulses, the selfishness and pleasure-seeking that drive us, even in recovery. Mindfulness meditation helps us to see these energies more clearly and let them go. Moving from Southern California to the Bay Area where there was more access to Buddhist teachers and community only served to strengthen this renewal and deepening of my practice.

In the Twelve Step literature, meditation is characterized as something that will help you maintain your recovery by helping you to access peace, intuition (called "God's will"), and inner strength. What I began to see was that the Buddhist teachings and practices gave me a much broader way of understanding the role of meditation in recovery. Today, I see meditation as a tool for working almost every step:

- When I sit down to practice, I see my own "powerlessness" over the arising of thoughts and sense experiences: Step One.

- When I see the effects of meditation, I begin to trust that my practice can have a significantly positive effect on my mind states: Step Two.

- When I commit to practice and learn to let go of the results of my time meditating, just accepting what comes up and watching it, I'm practicing Step Three.

- When all my stuff comes up—"the full catastrophe" —during meditation, I take a kind of inventory of my own heart/mind: Step Four.

- Step Five is essentially sharing my inventory. While this can't be done in the silence of meditation, I can do the other two parts of the Step: admit to God and to myself "the exact nature" of my stuff. (Although, I must admit, I don't quite know what it means to "admit to God" other than being honest to myself on the deepest level.)

- Just practicing meditation lays the groundwork for letting go: Step Six.

- My practice transforms me in many ways as I work at it, not through magic but through showing up and making skillful effort: Step Seven.

- The list of people I've harmed tends to show up in my meditation, especially in forgiveness and lovingkindness meditation: Step Eight.

- I can't make amends to others in silent meditation, though mindfulness and lovingkindness certainly help me to make those amends more skillfully. Nonetheless, I consider my meditation practice to be very healing for myself, and thus an amends to me: Step Nine.

- My daily meditation practice helps me to stay current with resentments and conflicts in my life: Step Ten.

- Step Eleven includes meditation and is the most direct connection to Buddhist practice.

- Step Twelve, which starts with a spiritual awakening, is founded in my spiritual growth, which, for me, is founded in meditation.

In short, I discovered that meditation isn't just a complement to my recovery program, or even just one little corner of it. It can be a pervasive tool for every Step.

Meditation and Joy

While meditation clearly has great value in the overall recovery process, it can take a special role in recovering joy. I'd like to explore a few of the ways that meditation can enhance our lives.

Quiet Time

As addicts, we were often in states of agitation and distress. Our minds tended to spin out with fear, resentment, grasping, and despair. Some of us used drugs and alcohol as a way to slow down, to kick back and relax. But rarely did this relaxation, which was really just intoxication, rejuvenate us in any way. At other times, we might have used stimulants that just spun things out further. The thing is, if we stopped to think or feel, the demons quickly overtook us, so our solution was to not stop, whether that meant a twenty-four-hour party life or obsessive working, or just constant distraction. The idea of stillness and inner peace, while sounding good, had no real place in our lives.

In recovery, many addicts still have trouble slowing down. Sometimes the same demons that dogged us in our addiction remain as persistent voices. We might find that going to lots of meetings, working a lot, and having a busy social life keep those demons at bay, but ultimately, without a path to inner quiet, we will struggle with these energies and be at more risk of relapse. When we are able to cultivate even a moderate meditation practice, we discover something else: just sitting still and quiet for a little while has a healing effect. We may not be able to stop our thoughts altogether, but just removing ourselves from the stresses and stimulations of our lives lets our nervous system calm down.

It's remarkable to me that even when my meditation seems completely filled with thoughts and worries and plans, at the end I feel a significant shift toward calm and clarity. Sometimes the things that come up are like little inventories or mindfulness bells, telling me what I need to do that day. At other times, I discover that something is troubling me that I wasn't even aware of. And many times, I realize that persistent thoughts in my mind are of very little importance, best ignored and forgotten. All of these effects trend toward stress reduction.

Quiet time lets me reflect on my life; it opens the creative channels; it softens my attitude toward myself and others; it reminds me what's important in life.

Present for the Richness of Life

One of the first meditation retreats I ever went on was in the high desert of Southern California. One day, after lunch, I was taking a walk amid the cactus and rocks. That spring, the desert was blooming as it does when there's been a wet winter. Here in this bleak, sandy landscape were stunning blossoms opening to the sun. I squatted down at one particularly beautiful cactus flower just to look closely. I watched as a parade of ants climbed into and then out of the inside of the plant, presumably drenching themselves in some sweet nectar. I found myself mesmerized by this scene, the beautiful colors, the persistence of life, and the moment in time when so many factors had come together to produce all this. For a long time, I just watched.

In the weeks after that retreat, I began to realize that the practice of mindfulness was making me aware of much more of life than I'd ever been. I realized that I'd never been very observant or appreciative of nature or my surroundings, and that my practice was opening me up to so much more of life. I felt more alive than ever.

Over the years, I've found it so valuable to be able to call upon the power of mindfulness to enrich my life. Every activity, from washing the dishes to making love, from talking to a friend to listening to music, is enhanced by paying attention more closely.

It's so interesting how we can try to find life in our heads—as though just thinking about things was enough to bring meaning. What the practice of mindfulness is showing us is that the richness of life is all around us if we allow ourselves to be touched by it.

Meditative Joy

When talking about joy in meditation, we can't overlook the deep states of concentration called *jhana,* or meditative absorption. The Buddha says that these states are the most pleasurable ones outside of transformative insights. The jhanas include two obviously pleasant experiences: *piti,* or rapture; and *sukha,* or joy. These come about in the process of deepening concentration that, for most people, can only be developed in longer silent retreats of two weeks or more (for most people, it's more). Piti is primarily characterized by intense physical states that come in different forms: bolts of energy surging through the body, flowing sensations of pleasure, chakra-opening bursts, and other remarkable states. These experiences have been documented in many religious traditions for millennia. While different traditions give different explanations and definitions of these states, Buddhism sees them in fairly simple terms as natural outgrowths of concentration.

Sukha is more of an emotional experience than piti, a warm, flowing state of well-being. It arises in the development of jhana after we have established piti. Resting in sukha gives a sense of peace and happiness beyond any normal experience. In fact, piti, sukha, and all the elements of jhana practice are actually altered states, reminiscent of normal pleasant states, but transcendent in their manifestation, truly beyond common human experience.

Meditative joy is something to be appreciated and even cultivated, as long as it doesn't become the sole purpose of our meditation. The Buddha says that jhana, while a remarkable and beautiful experience, is really only important for the concentration it enables that allows us to go to deeper levels of insight. He recommended developing jhana as a tool for awakening, but warned against diverting our practice into a pursuit of these pleasurable states. Like all experiences, they are impermanent. While they can be established on retreat, and sustained for some time in daily life with determined practice, most laypeople can't maintain them permanently. In order to truly enjoy life, the Buddha tells us, we must develop the art and grace of being fully present while being ready to let go of each moment as it passes.

Opening the Heart

When I went on my first meditation retreat, I expected to come out of it in a state of bliss—probably imagining something like jhana states. However, my practice wasn't developed enough to arrive at those levels of concentration, and instead, I spent the week after the retreat lapsing into periods of crying, something I hadn't done in many years. I was surprised and disappointed, and even wrote a song called "Vipassana Blues" to try to describe the experience. A friend who had some experience in spiritual work told me that what was happening was that "my heart was opening." I didn't know exactly what this meant, but it at least gave me a more hopeful and positive way of viewing what until then had seemed like a failure of my practice.

Although I've never specifically seen Buddhist texts that referred to an experience like this, there seem to be generally accepted stages of spiritual opening that many people experience across traditions. Certainly the idea of a connection between love, spiritual growth, and the physical center of the chest is a common one. As this happened for me, a new sensitivity arose. A sense of connection with others, with nature, and with the universe revealed itself; an appreciation of beauty grew; the ability to care about and be compassionate toward others' suffering also grew. In this opening, there was the realization of how closed I had been for many years. I had been afraid to feel, afraid of other people's pain, afraid to love and be loved—and all of these fears had run like white noise in the background of my heart/mind. This opening is one of the most precious aspects of spiritual growth. It's not simply a happy experience, because it allows in the totality of life, both good and bad, but it is a rich experience, one that makes us feel more fully alive, not cut off from any aspect of life.

In the Buddhist world, there are many popular teachings on how to cultivate and sustain the open heart. The metta, or lovingkindness, practice is now a primary practice for many people. What I discovered on that first retreat is that metta arises naturally out of mindfulness. The openness that comes with mindfulness practice lets in—and out—the lovingkindness that is metta. Either way, through intentional cultivation or just through mindfulness, these practices incline toward the joy of an open heart.

The Joy of Insight

Though the Buddha spends a lot of time talking about the dangers of craving and clinging, it's interesting that he doesn't altogether demonize pleasure. He says that it's fine to enjoy the sense world as long as we don't get attached—or addicted. Obviously, this is a big challenge, but mindfulness can really help us in this enterprise. First, it allows us to be fully present for and enjoy a moment of sense pleasure. And second, it helps us to let go of the experience as it passes.

While the Buddha doesn't discount sense pleasure, he does put it at the bottom of his hierarchy of pleasure. Above it is meditative joy—which includes jhana, heart practice, and any moment of comfort that comes in meditation. And above meditative joy is the joy of insight or wisdom. The highest form of insight is enlightenment.

The term *insight*, or *vipassana*, is easily misunderstood because in our culture insight usually refers to a thought, some realization that we can verbalize. Insight in Buddhist terms is an *experience*, and isn't always understood or even noticed at the moment, but may become clearer over time. One of the key insights in Buddhism comes when we see and feel how many forms of thought are painful, and that stopping or letting go of these thoughts is a relief. This is, essentially, insight into the second and third Noble Truths. We don't have to think about this to know it; we just have to experience it. And most people who have done any amount of meditation have had this experience. In that moment of letting go, there is a great sense of relief. When, further, we come to understand this insight, it gives us clear guidance for our intention in our lives—that if we want to be happy, we need to see where we are getting caught and let go. This is the foundation insight to all of Buddhism.

This is also the foundation insight of recovery: when we stop being attached to our drug or behavior of choice, we begin our journey of freedom. What's important is that we *see* these things, these insights. While we might experience them, if we aren't paying attention and making note of them, we may not fully absorb them. This is why mindfulness is so important in recovery and in finding joy. I didn't truly see that clinging to drugs and alcohol was the cause of my suffering before I got sober, and I've seen many people who are on the fence about recovery who hadn't fully accepted this for themselves. The power and seduction of addiction tend to obscure the truth, to limit our capacity to make the connection between our clinging and our suffering. We can continue to believe that there is something there for us in our addictive behavior.

Insight into how suffering arises and how it passes is one of the three core insights, called the Three Characteristics, that the Buddha pointed to as gateways to wisdom and freedom. Each of these motivates us to let go.

Another characteristic is impermanence. The Buddha points over and over at the importance of seeing how everything is constantly changing. While this may seem obvious, most of us don't live as though we know it. We're surprised when signs of aging appear, when our parents die, when our kids grow up—maybe not surprised, but somehow not really prepared. We want the safety of a static, stable world, and our minds perceive things as solid. We need this perception to some extent just to function, but living under that illusion eventually backfires as the truth inevitably overturns our perception. When we make the shift into seeing impermanence clearly, we naturally are more present for life. We see that there is nothing to hold on to, so we let go with more grace. We appreciate what is here now, knowing full well that it will disappear, if not sooner, then later. We begin to live in harmony with the ever-changing flow of life.

Insight into not-self, the third Characteristic, is subtler. This comes from seeing that if everything is in constant motion, then what I call "I" is also just a mix of ever-changing elements. There's no solid or stable essence. While this can seem disorienting, once it's understood, there is a natural peace that comes, as we realize that what we have felt the need to build up and defend is just a thought in our mind, an image of selfness that has no substance.

PRACTICE   **Deepening Concentration**

Concentration is one of the most difficult aspects of meditation to develop. It takes time and patience, both of which can be hard to find. Many concentration practices are also somewhat boring, at least to me. Each of the following practices uses the breath. Remember that whatever else you are doing, part of any breath practice is to *feel the actual sensations,* not just count or repeat the phrases.

Counting breaths: There are a couple approaches to this, usually counting to ten. Pa-Auk Sayadaw recommends eight, because it's easy to hypnotically count to ten. He suggests counting in the small space between the end of the outbreath and the beginning of the next inbreath. Other approaches count during the inbreath or during the outbreath. I suggest you try different variations and see what works for you. The idea is that if you lose track or start spacing out, you go right back to one and start again.

I have my own version of this—totally unapproved by other teachers—in which you just keep counting, trying to get to one hundred. I don't worry if I space out or even if I lose count; I just pick it up wherever I think I left off, and keep going. Usually I find that by seventy or so, my mind has settled down. Many people would consider this a sloppy approach, tantamount to cheating—maybe that's why I like it.

Detailed breath: In this approach, you try to notice at least three different sensations on each inbreath and three sensations on each outbreath. This forces you to pay close attention and tends to shut out thoughts. This approach to noticing details can work with any of the five senses—for instance, listening closely to sounds or paying close attention to the sensations in the body.

Gathas: I've used and taught this practice from Thich Nhat Hanh many times. Here you repeat words with the breath. There are five phrases, which can be cycled through one after the other, or else you can stay on one phrase for several minutes before moving on to the next one:

> In, Out
> Deep, Slow
> Calm, Ease
> Smile, Release
> Present Moment, Wonderful Moment.

Don't think about the meaning of the words, but do let their meaning come through and resonate within you. ▪

Brahmaviharas: Four Aspects of Heart Opening

As I've already talked about, heart opening is one of the most precious results of meditation practice and spiritual growth. The Buddhist path

THE FOUR BRAHMAVIHARAS

Metta, or Lovingkindness, is the quality of wishing happiness for others and ourselves.

Karuna, or Compassion, is the quality of caring about the suffering of others and ourselves.

Mudita, or Sympathetic Joy, is the quality of appreciating and being happy for the happiness of others.

Upekkha, or Equanimity, is the quality of mental balance and peace that allows us to feel each of the other three qualities without getting swept away or lost in clinging or aversion.

presents four different aspects of this process—four different practices and viewpoints that are valuable in cultivating joy and balance in our lives. These four are called Brahmaviharas, or "Divine Abodes." They are the highest emotions—heavenly states of heart and mind.

The Buddha encourages us in some of his suttas to make positive wishes for all beings, and these wishes have been turned into systematic practices by various commentators and teachers both recent and ancient. Here, I think it's best if I admit that I've never used these practices as a primary meditation form or done a whole retreat devoted to them. Mostly I have done shorter periods of lovingkindness meditation, which I find powerful and rewarding. The one time I tried to do a "Metta Retreat," though, I wound up debating with the teacher about what phrases I should use, and simply got frustrated trying to constantly use the phrases over the two-week retreat. Nonetheless, I know that for many, many people, these practices have been transforming and become a primary type of meditation.

And I do use these teachings and practices on a daily basis. In fact, I find them tremendously helpful and inspiring guidelines for living in the world. For me, it's the spirit of lovingkindness, compassion, sympathetic joy, and equanimity that I'm most interested in. I want to bring these qualities into my life and into my attitude toward others. If you are interested in pursuing these practices in a formal way, read Sharon Salzberg's *Lovingkindness* and Noah Levine's *The Heart of the Revolution*. Both of these books outline these practices beautifully. Further, to get the best guidance, find a teacher who can guide you with these practices. Most teachers use phrases for lovingkindness, but Ayya Khema, the late Buddhist nun, presented a unique way of doing metta using visualization and feelings. You can find her approach in some of her books and in the teachings of her senior student, Leigh Brasington.

Meanwhile, I'll do my best here to explain these states and the practices that go with them.

Metta (Lovingkindness)

Metta (lovingkindness) is that sense of openness when we feel connected to everyone and everything in the world. In some ways, it's a natural outgrowth of mindfulness practice and just the general cultivation of happiness in our lives. When the Buddha talks about lovingkindness, he's clearly pointing to something different from what we usually call "love." In fact, his teachings point to the problems with selective love, and how that leads to clinging and ultimately suffering as things change. The Metta Sutta tells us to spread love over the entire world to everyone, no matter what we think or feel about them. This is unconditional love, love that doesn't expect or need a return, love that sees past the petty differences and disputes in life to the universal longings for happiness that we all share. In practicing lovingkindness, we are faced with our clinging, our judgments, and our selective caring. We see that what we usually call love may have a lot of conditions tied up with it: "I'll love you as long as you love me" or "as long as you give me what I want." And, further, we see that the love we have for our dear ones makes us vulnerable to grief and loss.

Traditionally, metta practice focuses on three categories: those we love, those we are neutral or have no strong feelings about, and those we have difficulties with. Before we work with these categories, the practice suggests we first focus on a benefactor or beloved person (or even a pet). When we spend time "sending" lovingkindness to this beloved, we accomplish a couple of things: first, we soften ourselves up a bit, so that we are ready to send love to others; and second, we get a clear sense of what love feels like so that we establish that kind of baseline.

After connecting with the beloved, we then try to send love to ourselves. Many people find this to be one of the most difficult aspects of the metta practice. At least in our culture, many of us have complicated, and often negative, feelings about ourselves. To see ourselves as just another person deserving of love is a valuable exercise. Here we start to disidentify with ourselves, see ourselves in more objective terms. When we can see ourselves as just another imperfect human, equally deserving of love as anyone else, it becomes easier to offer love to ourselves.

Moving from focus on ourselves to focus on all the rest of the people we care about—family, friends, intimates, and partner—the heart tends to open more easily. Now we might feel ourselves getting into the flow of lovingkindness. Without obstruction, and using the phrases, feelings, and visualizations of the practice, the mind can become quite focused and concentrated, so that not only do we enjoy the pleasant feeling of love, but also the powerful feeling of concentration, called *samadhi,* that comes with deeper meditation practices.

We then try to carry these two qualities, the openheartedness and the focus, into giving metta to a "neutral" person or persons. For many people, this seems to be an awkward practice at first, but I think it has great potential in terms of growing a broad sense of lovingkindness for all beings.

A neutral person is someone we don't have strong feelings about, either positive or negative. I've used people like the clerk in the video store and the security guard at the bank. These are people I can visualize pretty easily because I've seen them many times, but I certainly don't like or dislike them in any meaningful way.

At first, and naturally enough, it might be hard to feel much about these people, but the practice gives us a form we can simply follow without worrying about the results. You see the person in your mind, you say the lovingkindness phrases to yourself, and you try to connect in your heart. What helps me in doing this practice is contemplating the universal desire for happiness and freedom from suffering. Even though I don't really know this neutral person, I know that, just like me, they want happiness. So, in a sense, I'm connecting with my own wish for happiness and just projecting it onto them.

As we work with the neutral person, we have the opportunity to see what the Buddha was getting at. It might be easy to wish happiness for your loved ones, but as you wish that, it's still very personal for you. You have some investment in their happiness, so it's difficult to disidentify with their happiness. However, with the neutral person, you have no investment, so you have to connect with something else, this universal longing that is impersonal. That moves you away from your self-identification into a more authentic metta. As long as there is identification or longing or investment in someone else's happiness, we aren't experiencing unconditional love.

I think that many people can get caught up in the idea that metta is about feeling good and praying for people you care about. This is something of a distortion of the teachings. Yes, being immersed in metta is a pleasant experience, but that experience isn't the goal of the practice.

Working with the difficult person makes this fact clear. If we were just trying to feel good, we certainly wouldn't spend time thinking about someone we don't like. The difficult person can be someone you've had conflict with or toward whom you have a resentment. Sometimes when no one in my life comes up, I just use a political figure that I disagree with. In any case, this is a place where we have to apply a strong mindfulness to our practice so that we don't lapse into aversion, anger, judgment, or resentment. As we follow through on the practice, visualizing the person and saying the phrases, it's very likely that we will not feel much that's positive, at least in our initial efforts. We need to be careful that the mind doesn't wander into negative thoughts and that we just keep with the simple task of the practice, staying with the words and the breath in the heart. Here, you may be able to get some insight into the limits of your own capacity for love. That's a valuable thing to see. It can give us some goals as well as show us where some of our own suffering comes from.

Clearly, the great spiritual masters believe that the capacity to love our enemies is one of the vital tasks of human evolution. Jesus spoke of this and exemplified it when he forgave those who crucified him; the Buddha explains this in the "Simile of the Saw," in which he says that even if someone were sawing off our limbs one by one, no thought of hatred should arise. If we want to be truly loving people, unconditionally and for all beings, we have to work with some form of this practice. It's certainly not something that I've come anywhere close to mastering, but I have found that with compassion practice, I can get some sense of this.

After working with the difficult person, we can move to the expansive part of metta practice. This is actually a complete shift because no longer are we thinking about any individuals, but working instead with a sense of space. This space is what the Buddha is talking about in the Metta Sutta when he says that we are "radiating kindness over the entire world, spreading upwards to the skies and downwards to the depths, outwards and unbounded, free from hatred and ill will."

This is a somewhat more difficult area of practice to describe because it doesn't have the same cognitive elements of the earlier pieces. Instead, we are working more with a feeling, a feeling of expansiveness and connection. Hopefully when we arrive at this part of the practice, we've developed something of an internal sense of lovingkindness. While focusing on that feeling, that authentic wish for all beings to be free from dukkha, or suffering, we begin a process of imaginative expansion. We can use a visualization if that works, while we stay connected to the feeling in the heart and imagine that the love is growing.

First we see/feel that love filling and enveloping the room we are in. Then we let that feeling expand out through the whole building, the neighborhood, outward in all directions until it touches everything on Earth. This can be done slowly or quickly, depending upon how much time you have and how into it you are. You can think of specific groups of people you want to send love to: the sick and dying, the oppressed, or whatever comes up for you. You can also send love to animals and plants and the earth itself.

At this point, you may lose the sense of boundaries with your body, and experience a sort of floating or fluid sensation. I'm not trying to tell you how you should feel—just know that anything in this realm is normal and helps to support this part of the practice. When we've spread lovingkindness over the entire planet, we then expand into space, vast and limitless. We try to permeate the universe with lovingkindness.

Once we've sat in this place of boundless love for a little while, we can bring ourselves gradually back into the body and heart and close the period of meditation.

The practice of spaciousness and boundlessness is useful beyond the metta practice. In jhana practice, this is similar to the spatial sense we develop in the higher jhanas, particularly in the Realm of Infinite Space, the fifth jhana. Cultivating this quality in metta practice gives us a taste or hint of what the fifth jhana is like, although the jhanas are altered states that actually take us out of any normal realm of consciousness. But in terms of cultivating these deeper concentration states, metta is a good doorway.

The sense of universal connection that comes from this expansive metta practice also helps us to understand the teachings on interdependence and not-self. We *feel* this interconnection, and we sense the falseness of ego boundaries.

PRACTICE Metta Phrases

I've more or less outlined the practice above. Always start by connecting with the breath, so you have some attention in your body, preferably at the heart. As I've said, we first send metta to a beloved person or benefactor, then ourselves, our dear ones, a neutral person, a difficult person, then radiating to all beings. A big part of this, then, is the felt sense of lovingkindness; however, this feeling may be stronger or weaker or even absent at times. Nonetheless, we continue the practice by visualizing the people we are sending metta to, maybe naming them, and repeating phrases. You should use phrases that resonate for you and are simple and direct. Not more than four phrases. Here are some typical ones:

May you be happy.

May you be peaceful.

May you live with ease.

Some people like to add something like, "May you be safe."

Stay in touch with your breath; notice feelings of happiness or resistance that come up at various stages; let the phrases flow with the breath and stay connected to the heart. ■

PRACTICE **Metta Visualization**

With this practice, taught by Ayya Khema, instead of using words, we use an image, like a beam of light that radiates from the heart. We then go through the same process of sending love to all the categories.

You first imagine that in your heart there is a beautiful white lotus flower with its petals closed. Gradually, as you breathe, the petals peel back, and a golden light shines forth.

Then have a sense that the golden light is radiating outward and shining on each category: the beloved, yourself, dear ones, neutral people, and difficult people.

After this, begin to radiate the golden light out in all directions, gradually expanding until the whole universe is filled with this light, which you can feel coming from your heart.

Finally, come back into the room, into your body and your breath. Seeing the golden light come back into your heart, you can get the sense that this limitless lovingkindness lives in your own heart and is always there, available to you if you just open to it.

The advantage of this form of metta practice is that it doesn't get the mind wrapped up in words, but stays more on the felt level. ■

Karuna (Compassion)

The next of the Brahmaviharas, *karuna,* or compassion, shifts our perspective subtly from wishing happiness for others to wishing them to be free from suffering. There are many benefits and much value in practicing compassion, but from the perspective of finding joy in our recovery, I think it's especially valuable in changing our perspective on others. This can happen when we begin to look at things from someone else's point of view, particularly from their suffering. I gained some insight into this on an early retreat when one of the hundred-plus participants was swallowing repeatedly in the silence of the meditation hall. I found the sound distracting and unpleasant and wished he (or she) would stop. When the subject of this person's swallowing came up the next day in a group interview with Jack Kornfield, he said that instead of being angry or judgmental toward this person, we should consider that they certainly didn't want to be swallowing and that this sometimes happened to people on a retreat—that they couldn't stop swallowing and that it was unpleasant when it happened to you. He suggested we send compassion to this person for their suffering. This was a big revelation for me. I realized how self-centered I'd been and saw how this shift in perspective completely changed my experience.

A few years later, I got a similar lesson from my boss when I was working for a magazine distributor. My boss's accountant often spoke negatively and angrily, and one day I mentioned to my boss how annoying I found this. My boss said that he handled it by realizing that if the accountant spoke this way out loud, then he probably spoke the same way to himself, berating and judging himself, and that that must be very painful. Instead of being frustrated with him, my boss said he felt compassion for him.

These two experiences really helped me to see how compassion could help me not to get so caught up in my own judgments and resentments. Clearly, compassion is the appropriate response to someone who is in obvious physical or mental pain, but to also be able to bring compassion to people whose behavior is irritating to you is more of a challenge—though it's equally, if not more, valuable.

PRACTICE   Sending Compassion

Compassion practice follows the same form as metta, just using different phrases. You can also choose to do compassion practice for particular people you know are suffering or in difficulty.

Here are some possible phrases:

I care about your pain.

May you be free from suffering.

When I do this practice for specific people who are ill, I say, "May you be healed." ▪

Mudita (Sympathetic Joy)

Mudita, or sympathetic joy, is, I suppose, the most obscure of the Brahmaviharas. It means that we "take joy in the joy of others." Simply understood, this is the opposite of envy or jealousy, and I think it's meant to be an antidote to them. It's said that if you practice mudita, you'll always have the opportunity to be happy because there's always *someone* whose joy you can share. This is probably beyond most of us—certainly me—but the idea of taking joy is a very helpful one.

As I've tried to bring this practice into my life, it's helped me to see how I often have a choice in how I respond to situations. When a friend tells me how they've achieved something that I've always wanted to achieve, there's that moment when I wish it were me—or at least not them. But with the view of mudita, I'm sometimes able to see that I also feel something else: happiness for my friend. When I see that, I can focus on the positive intentionally, and let the envy move to the background.

Another translation of *mudita* is "appreciative joy," and I find this helpful in broadening the meaning. Appreciation can be about nature or anything positive in our lives; it can blend into gratitude. It is the basis for the "OPT" practice I offered in chapter 1. With mudita, I'll simply make the intentional effort at times to notice if there is anything around me right now I can enjoy, or if there is anything in the situation I'm in that I can be grateful for. This opens up many possibilities for moments of joy.

PRACTICE **Appreciative Joy**

The phrases for mudita are about hoping that someone's happiness continues and grows:

May your happiness continue.

May your happiness grow.

For me, this is a practice I use more in daily life—when I'm happy for someone, when I see a happy child, or when I get some good news about someone. I simply try to fully feel that happiness. On those occasions when I feel envy arising, I try to shift toward mudita. ■

Upekkha (Equanimity)

The fourth Brahmavihara, *upekkha,* was apparently the one most valued by the Buddha. It appears as the final factor in the Seven Factors of Enlightenment, and it embodies the highest form of emotional happiness that the Buddha praised: peace. I've found, though, that there is a lot of confusion about the term. Some people think it is a form of passivity or apathy, while others think it sounds boring or dull, and not joyful at all. In fact, equanimity, as the Buddha is talking about it, is a perfect balance of mind: open, caring, present; calm, undisturbed, clearheaded. A state of pure awareness that allows for the arising of wisdom, intuition, and creativity. Equanimity is the capacity to be fully engaged in all three of the other Brahmaviharas without clinging, aversion, or delusion. In other words, when practicing metta, our wish for others to be happy can cross over into a state of desire and grasping. But equanimity protects us from that by being clear about the danger of being overinvested in results. When practicing karuna, our concern for others can turn into pity or a wish to turn away—aversion—but equanimity helps us to hold their suffering with balance, openness, and courage. When practicing mudita, we can become caught up in an unrealistically positive view of the world—Pollyannalike—but, again, equanimity keeps us clear-eyed and realistic.

Equanimity is a state of emotional balance and meditative stability. It is one of the results of determined and sustained meditation practice, and it's founded in clearly seeing reality, the Dharma. One of the classic ways of developing equanimity is to observe what's called *vedana,* the immediate impact of each sense and mind experience. The word *vedana* is translated as "feeling"—however, it doesn't refer to emotion, but rather to the pleasant, unpleasant, or neutral quality each sense impression conveys to us. Normally we don't notice these effects as such, but tend to just react to them, clinging to the pleasant, rejecting the unpleasant, and brushing aside the neutral. These reactions are what lead to suffering, as described in the second Noble Truth. When, instead of falling prey to these reactions, we can simply see the vedana, we interrupt the movement toward suffering, and settle back into the peace of equanimity.

Of course, seeing these immediate impressions requires a lot of mindfulness and concentration. The only time I've been able to track them closely is on retreat. Mostly what I do is notice *after* I've reacted: "Oh, that pleasant experience got me," or, "That was really unpleasant; no wonder I got irritated." While this isn't perfect, it certainly helps in our efforts to attain some equanimity in our lives.

PRACTICE **Balanced Mind**

As I've said, equanimity pulls us back from being attached to the results of our other Brahmavihara practices, and the traditional phrase that goes with it explains how that works: "All beings are the owners of their karma. Their happiness or unhappiness depends on their actions, not on my wishes for them."

More than a meditative mantra, I see these words as a valuable reflection. This resonates with Step Three of the Twelve Steps: we are turning the results of our wishes over to a Higher Power, the Power of Karma. This lets us know that the metta practices are not magic and that we aren't responsible. If something bad happens to someone we've done metta for, it's not because we didn't do the practice right or long or hard enough. They are responsible, as far an anyone is uniquely responsible, for the outcome of their lives. ∎

A Power Greater Than Ourselves

In the recovery world, there's a lot of discussion of the idea of Higher Power and of God. I remember once going to a "We Agnostics" meeting in LA, expecting to hear about different ways of relating to the Steps. Instead, the whole meeting seemed to be taken up with people debating and complaining about God. Kind of like a men's meeting spending all the time talking about women.

I've personally found the subject of Higher Power to be an interesting one, and my book *A Burning Desire* explores this pretty thoroughly from a Buddhist perspective, so I won't attempt to reiterate everything I said there. Rather, what I'd like to talk about is how *some* kind of connection with *something* outside of us can bring joy and release to our lives.

It's a terrible burden to feel alone and isolated in the world. Many addicts experience this, especially in the depths of their addiction. We all want love and connection, but many of us have a hard time finding those things. This isn't about personal relationships, which I've already explored, but rather something we might call "our place in the world." And it's not about "believing in God," a concept that I find somewhat odd. It's more about our inner life, how we feel in relation to the world.

Certainly, many people feel they have a personal connection with God. But I've also heard people say they've lost their connection to God. For me, that points to the idea that feelings are very changeable: one day you feel connected to God, and the next day you don't. Certainly we can cultivate the feeling of connection, and that's one of the significant effects of meditation and spiritual practice, but we need to understand that the *feeling* of connection will come and go. What we can rely on more, perhaps, is the *insight* into the ways we are connected.

Buddhism talks about this connection in terms of interdependence, our relationships to each other and to nature. We can see that we are part of nature, supported by nature and supporting it. Sadly, it's humans' sense of *not* being part of nature, of believing we can dominate nature, that has brought us to the brink of environmental disaster. So while feeling a connection with nature has a spiritual impact and benefit, acting and living on that basis have real-world implications.

Many spiritual teachers remind us of the importance of being in nature. Often, meditation centers and monasteries are in beautiful natural environments. For many of us, a simple walk in the woods or the hills or the meadows is uplifting and energizing. We don't have to build some philosophical or spiritual model to justify this feeling—we just experience it. When we sit by the ocean or gaze at the stars, we can see that we are small, that we are part of something vast. We are not separate from that, and knowing and sensing that connection is healing and comforting. This connection with nature and interdependence is one way we can sense something greater than us.

In the Twelve Steps, Higher Power is seen as a source of care, wisdom, and protection. The Buddhist corollary to this is to "Take Refuge in the Buddha, the Dharma, and the Sangha." When we take refuge, we are trusting in the power of these three to care for and guide us. Taking refuge is a devotional act, one of surrender, love, and commitment. We acknowledge that the Buddha himself transformed human history with his wisdom teachings; we strive to live like him, to embody the qualities of a Buddha. We devote ourselves to living in harmony with the Dharma, with the truth and the laws of the universe; we commit ourselves to living ethically, compassionately, and wisely. We go to the Sangha, the community, as a source of love and support and as a place to be of service. The Sangha is the living Dharma, the living Buddha, the place where the teacher and his teachings take form.

We can see how powerful many of the aspects of the Dharma are, and living in harmony with these powers is essentially how I view Step Three in the Twelve Steps—how we "turn our will and our lives over to the care of God." Living in harmony with the Law of Karma brings peace and safety to our lives. The power of mindfulness is transformative, giving us a whole different way of experiencing our lives and responding to the joy and challenges that come our way. And the Three Characteristics of Impermanence, Suffering, and Not-Self have a huge impact on our lives—and how we relate to them, either with acceptance and wisdom or resistance and denial, determines whether that impact is pleasant or unpleasant. Understanding the Four Noble Truths guides us in living happily; following the Eightfold Path brings integration and clarity; practicing lovingkindness enhances all of our interactions. In these ways, and many others, our understanding of the power of the Dharma and our capacity to live that understanding largely determine how happy we will be.

6

FOR THE FUN OF IT

finding our way back to play

Having fun is not a simple issue for people in recovery. Our so-called fun for many years involved doing the very thing we are now trying to stop doing. In recovery, the idea of having fun can seem dangerous or risky, like we somehow can't trust ourselves to let loose without losing control and relapsing. It can be easier to just focus on working on improving yourself and maintaining your recovery. At some point, though, the sense that all we are doing is working on ourselves can start to become burdensome. Isn't there more to life than work and meetings and constant self-improvement?

The time has arrived to start to look for activities that both absorb and feed us, be they hobbies, sports, artistic pursuits, or something else. Fun isn't something we do in order to accomplish something, to improve ourselves, to impress anyone, or to make money. Fun is something we do just to enjoy ourselves. A fun activity may be difficult and challenging within its own context and rules, but ultimately has no purpose or importance outside of the activity itself. That doesn't mean there are no peripheral benefits, like getting exercise, creating artwork, making new friends, or learning something new, but those benefits aren't the motivating impulse.

What Do You Enjoy?

When I was a kid, I loved sports. I played on the Little League team, I was on my high school wrestling team, and year-round I did everything from tennis and swimming to football, basketball, and track.

I had one game in which I bounced a tennis ball off the front steps of our house and went through the lineup of my favorite baseball team. The odd bounces from the steps would create the random plays of a baseball game.

My favorite thing, though, was to be out on the golf course on a sunny day with friends, or late on an autumn afternoon alone, the shadows stretching across the green as I putted to win the Masters.

When I think of my childhood, it's often memories of sports that come up. Those are happy memories. And yet, by the time I was seventeen and smoking pot every day, I had virtually stopped playing any sports. Once I became a musician, I left all that behind. Living in motels or shabby apartments, scratching and scraping to get by, there was no time for games other than the ones I'd watch on TV. I didn't have enough friends to get up a basketball game or the money to play golf. Not that it would have occurred to me. When I discovered drugs and alcohol, they became my "fun"—at least, that's what I thought they were. Originally they were part of my social life, but eventually they just became something like a prescription that was meant to sustain my mood and provide an instant escape. Playing golf or other sports didn't fit with my self-image as a cool, countercultural hero.

A big part of recovery for me was seeing that the identities I'd assumed—an outsider who had rejected his middle-class upbringing; a starving, undiscovered musician—didn't work for me anymore, and in fact, no longer made sense. Over the first few years of my recovery, these identities slowly crumbled and I started to be able to make decisions based on what might actually make me happy, rather than on fantasies or self-image. It has been this work and these decisions—the choices I've made around moral behavior, relationships, work, and all the rest— that ultimately led to this book,.

Over time, I've focused more specifically on happiness. A decade or so ago, I took a workshop with my teacher James Baraz called

"Awakening Joy." (He's subsequently published a book by the same name.) One of the first exercises he gave us was to write a list of things that made us happy. We weren't supposed to think too much or censor ourselves, just brainstorm for a few minutes. My list had everything from chocolate to meditation retreats, from making love to my wife to going to a ball game with my daughter. But one thing stood out for me: golf.

I felt a little embarrassed about that. It felt a little like a dirty secret. Golf is associated with a lot of things I don't want to be linked with: old, conservative white men, elitist country clubs, racism, sexism, and really ugly clothes. Despite all this, I knew that I wanted to play. As I explored my inner conflict, it was clear that a lot of my resistance to taking up the game again was my fear of what other people would think. Here I was a Buddhist meditation teacher living in Berkeley, radical capital of America, and I wanted to play golf. I should have been riding a bicycle, hiking, or doing yoga. Or maybe playing Ultimate Frisbee. While I have done these things (okay, not Ultimate Frisbee), none of them had a pull on me like golf. I figured that if I were sincere about this practice of "awakening joy," then I should try playing and see what happened. So I started dropping in at the local municipal course, borrowing clubs and hitting balls on the range. I could see right away that I was a long way from having a decent game. But the pull remained.

Eventually, I bought a cheap set of clubs and started playing on small nine-hole courses where I could start to get a feel for the game. Finally, I got up the nerve to play an eighteen-hole course. As I got to the first tee where two other men I'd been paired with were getting ready to tee off, I apologized, saying that I wasn't very good. They both laughed and said not to worry, that they weren't either. I felt a great relief, and soon discovered that this camaraderie and kindness were common on golf courses. That was almost five years ago. Today I feel really lucky that I have this activity that absorbs me, challenges me, is healthy, and gives me satisfaction and joy. It just shows the power of ego that it took me so long to come back to this game that I love.

James Baraz tells about how he had his own secret pleasure: watching professional football and rooting for his favorite team. He, too, as a Buddhist teacher, felt that he couldn't let his community know about this pleasure because of the violence and commercialization of football, its association with beer commercials, cheerleaders, and ritualistic spectacle. Eventually, though, he realized that he needed to be seen for who he was, and when he revealed his football obsession, he helped many people in his community let go of their own protective self-image. Certainly, it helped me to let go of my embarrassment about playing golf.

As addicts, many of us lost touch with the things that once made us happy, as we became more and more dependent on our drug or activity of choice and moved farther from the capacity to enjoy simple pleasures. While our recovery necessarily requires some tough work—letting go of our addiction, looking at our inventory, and making amends—if we're going to find a reason to embrace this new life, we'll also need to find things that make us happy. In chapter 9 ("What's the Plan?"), I'll give you more of a blueprint for this work, but right now I just want to emphasize the importance of the idea that recovery involves more than a struggle, and encourage you to see clearly the resistance and complications there might be in finding joy or pleasure outside of addiction so that you can begin to move toward a happier life.

REFLECTION **What Was Fun?**

Reflect on those playful activities you loved before you became an addict. What did you love to do when you were a kid? What did you give up once you took up your addiction? ■

REFLECTION **What Would You Do?**

Is there some playful activity you'd like to return to or take up but are afraid you'll be judged for doing? Maybe you are afraid of how it would look to others, or maybe it doesn't fit with your self-image. Is it worth it to let these things stand in the way of your fun? What are you protecting? What are you accomplishing with that stance? ∎

What Are You Afraid Of?

Recently, I found out that a new friend, a younger dharma teacher, had played a lot of golf when he was young. Since I have very few dharma friends who join me on the course, I invited him to play. At first he hesitated, but finally he agreed to go to the range and practice a bit.

As soon as I saw him strike the ball, I knew he was good. Very good. His ball soared out in a beautiful arc that mine never seem to achieve and went farther than my balls by miles. I couldn't believe that he'd apparently given up the sport by the time he graduated from college more than fifteen years earlier.

Later, as we did some putting, he told me about what was challenging for him about golf, how his competitiveness robbed him of the simple joy of playing, how the bad shots undermined his pleasure. I told him that I had the same tendency, but that my wife had told me that I wasn't "allowed to come home from golf in a bad mood," because I was going out to have fun. We both laughed over this advice and agreed that it was a pretty good suggestion.

Later, I started reflecting on my friend's difficulties and how he'd given up something he was really good at and must have loved at some point in his life. I thought about my own experiences of failure in organized sports, how I was a washout in Little League and the worst wrestler on the high school team, one season getting pinned in every match. I wondered if many of us take these childhood and adolescent scars with us into adulthood.

Two songs come to mind. The first, Janis Ian's "At Seventeen," is the poignant, painful story of a teenage outsider that includes the lines " . . . and those whose names were never called/When choosing sides for basketball." Isn't that the story for most of us—don't most of us at some point give up or never take up sports because we aren't good enough? I see it now with my own daughter who is a high school athlete. Sports become more and more competitive and selective the older we get; eventually, all except the elite athletes are eliminated from competition. Does that mean that each of these "rejects" carries some wound with them from their failure? I'm sure some are more able to hold those experiences wisely, but many of us, I suspect, just feel like losers.

The other song that I think of is Bruce Springsteen's "Glory Days," which has a verse about the hotshot high school pitcher who's now relegated to reliving what turned out to be the high point of his life. So even for the "winners," there's dukkha.

Adults often take part in sports that can be noncompetitive, like running or biking. Maybe this allows them the joy without the stress. The more solitary pursuits, like golf, also don't require getting a group together—something that's much easier to do with a gang of neighborhood kids than with a bunch of busy adults. Still, I remember a few years ago playing a softball game with some other parents of the kids on my daughter's softball team. A fly ball came my way, and a feeling of absolute panic came over me. In those few seconds, all the confidence that I normally felt when playing catch with my daughter dissolved. I fully expected to miss the ball and to be humiliated in front of the others. Somehow I caught it, but that feeling was enough to convince me that joining an adult softball team was not in my future.

Similar fears can attack us around artistic play. Maybe you'd love to start painting or throwing pots but are afraid of producing rubbish. A creative-writing class might sound like fun, but you're afraid you'll discover that you have no talent.

I've been on the outside of this kind of discomfort when people ask me for guitar lessons. I see how adults who try to pick up an instrument start with an incredibly negative self-view: "You're so good, and I'm so bad. You have talent, and I don't." When I learned guitar at twelve years old, no such thoughts occurred to me. But as adults, I think we aren't used to being beginners and having to go through the difficult process of learning a new skill. We're much more comfortable being experts. We work at a job we're experienced with; we know much more than our kids and can teach them things; we can drive a car, make a meal, and do all the things involved with being an adult.

Each of us has our special skills like carpentry or writing or computer programming, but most of us have quit learning new things.

Recovery is often a moment in adulthood when we are once again willing to be beginners. It's a surrender to the failure of our life strategy, and if things go well, we become open to new strategies and new ways of living. That's when a door can open on learning, again, how to have fun. Our inventory or some other stage of our recovery may uncover the wounds of not being chosen at basketball or being stuck in past glories, and help us to move past those old stories into new possibilities.

The idea that having fun as an adult can have all these complications and implications strikes me as ironic. Self-consciousness, self-judgment, regrets, and longing can make this simple idea a problem.

Perhaps the greatest fear in this regard for people in recovery is returning to activities that were part of their addiction. For me this was music. For about two decades, any time I rehearsed, performed, or wrote a song, I was high, and often enough drinking as well. I was fortunate that I was able to keep playing without relapsing after I got sober, but I know many other musicians who have struggled with their relationship to performing clean and sober. Lots of alcoholics have never gone to a ball game sober or watched the Super Bowl without a drink. Even eating a pizza can trigger the craving for a beer. Going fishing or to the beach or the lake, playing poker with the boys or having dinner with friends, seeing a concert or having sex—any of these activities and many others can be associated with our addiction. Some people find that the first time they do one of these things sober is a joyful revelation. Others activities might seem awkward and alien. Obviously, we need to take care that we don't get triggered to relapse, but if we avoid every activity we ever did when loaded, we're going to be living a pretty narrow existence. And, often enough, we discover that the drink or drug that we thought was enhancing our experience was actually blurring it.

As we begin to build a joyful life in recovery, these are the opportunities and challenges that we face. Each of us must make choices about which past activities to revive and which ones to drop, which new experiences we'd like to try and which fears we are willing to face. Fun and play may seem trivial, but a happy, healthy life depends to some degree on our integration of them into our lives.

REFLECTION **Being a Beginner**

What new activity would you love to try even though it might mean becoming a beginner again or having to start a whole new learning curve? How do you feel when you think about starting as a beginner? Is there a feeling of excitement at the thought of learning something new, a thrill at the thought of working to master a new skill or activity? Or does your ego jump in and try to talk you out of it? ◼

REFLECTION **Being Imperfect**

Are there any activities in your life that you do even though you perceive yourself to be "not very good" at them? What can you do to make peace with being "not very good" at them—or at least not good at them right now? If you can't get past your own self-judgment and competitiveness, consider doing things where good and bad aren't a question, like hiking, walking, playing with a dog or other pet, or going to a concert or sporting event. ◼

7

HEALTH AND WEALTH

taking care of our bodies
and our bank accounts

Everyone wants to be healthy and financially secure. Those are natural desires, and it's not unreasonable to think we need those things in order to be happy. Unfortunately, as the Buddha points out, everyone gets sick, and with aging our bodies and health inevitably decline. As for finances, the teaching on impermanence makes clear that security is an illusion; no one is safe from the vicissitudes of economics. No, we can't depend on health and wealth, and in fact, happiness *doesn't* depend on them. Rather it's our *relationship* to our health and our bodies and our *relationship* to our financial situation that are more important in determining how happy we are.

In our addiction, we may have a cavalier or irresponsible relationship toward our bodies and our bank accounts. Hangovers are just the price we pay for what we feel like we need to do. Money? Well, it's just there to serve our cravings.

When we get clean, we're often faced with the results of these unwise choices and actions. In the early years of recovery, many of us face tremendous challenges around money and health. As we rebuild our lives, we may have to rebuild our bodies and our finances. After that, though, we are faced with the challenges that everyone—and not just addicts—faces: the challenges of living with a body and dealing with money.

Healing

In her book *How to Be Sick,* Toni Bernhard tells the story of her journey with chronic fatigue syndrome. Struck down out of the blue in the midst of an active life and successful academic career, Toni found herself physically incapable of getting out of bed, completely incapacitated. Not surprisingly, she fell into despair, self-pity, and passive resignation. With a background in Buddhist practice, she eventually started to change her relationship to her illness. This wasn't just a matter of looking on the bright side or letting go of aversion. This was—and still is for her—deep spiritual practice, with all its attendant challenges. She works at balancing Right Effort with letting go, because doing too much wears her out, but doing nothing makes her sink. She works at seeing her illness as impersonal, "not I, me, or mine." She practices mindfulness, watching her thoughts, watching her sensations, and trying not to become attached to the negative or unpleasant. She cultivates calm and concentration to bring more peace, acceptance, and serenity. And *she wrote a book* about all of this. All of these actions and nonactions are shifts away from viewing illness as something inherently bad and limiting to her happiness. And none of it has taken her illness away. Yet she is healed.

What do I mean by that?

My friend and colleague Dr. Paul Epstein, an integrative medical practitioner, has made it his primary purpose to help people understand the difference between healing and getting rid of a disease or condition ("getting well"). He points to the root of the words *health* and *healing,* which is *whole.* Healing, according to Dr. Epstein, isn't about getting well, but about becoming whole with whatever our condition is. We tend, as he points out, to think of an illness as separate from us: "I *have* this condition and I want to get rid of it." This sense of separation creates an internal conflict for us, a split in our being that causes suffering, dukkha. Rather, he says, healing is about changing our relationship to our condition—not necessarily being happy about it, but not being in conflict. When there is this sense of acceptance, many possibilities open up. With rejection, there is only one possibility: push it away. With openness, there is the possibility of seeing opportunity or challenge in our condition; there is the possibility of *working with* our limitations or struggles. We can learn to be mindful and fully experience our condition instead of always trying to marginalize it. We can develop compassion for ourselves and others who suffer as we do; we can share our struggle with others.

My own most difficult physical challenge has been dealing with back pain. It started seemingly out of the blue almost twenty years ago. Drying myself off after a shower, I suddenly felt a stab of pain and clenching muscles in my lower back that made me collapse to the floor of my apartment. I crawled to the bed and managed to pull myself up so I could lie down. I lay there in shock. What was happening? What should I do? The confusion and fear were just as much of a problem as the pain itself. I was in the last semester of graduate school, a very stressful time in my life, and later on I would realize how integral that stress had been to this occurrence. For a dozen years, I tried to fix my back problems. After the most excruciating attack of all, I explored every treatment I could: medication, physical therapy, chiropractic, acupuncture, cortisone injections. I discussed surgery with a doctor, but decided against it. Many treatments helped temporarily, but most, including even the lightest forms of physical therapy, actually aggravated the problem.

One thing that happens when you have a problem like this is that your friends and acquaintances want to help, so they all share their solutions. People told me what caused back pain, how to fix it, what I shouldn't do, and what I should do. They recommended books, therapists, doctors; exercises, drugs, and treatments. Some I tried and some I ignored.

Finally I gave up—and that's when I started to get better. In my case, I found what I most needed was rest and relaxation: to do nothing. I took up crossword puzzles. Slowly, I returned to gentle activity, mostly taking walks and doing a very abbreviated set of yoga poses. I found that there were some things I simply couldn't do: Running, for instance, triggered serious back spasms within twenty-four hours. And rigorous yoga didn't work. But I could walk and I could ride a bike. Later, I found I could play golf, which may be counterintuitive given the back twists involved in swinging a club. And I found that regularly doing my short yoga routine helped keep me pain free. I realized that I had my own unique problems and needs, and that I needed to trust my own solutions and develop my own plan.

Still, most days I wake up with back pain because lying down for long stretches aggravates it. And walking eighteen holes of golf often requires ibuprofen, while sitting too long, like when I'm on an airplane or at a movie, tightens the muscles until they become painful. What do I do about all this pain? I try to accept it. Having spent hours working with difficult sensations in sitting meditation, I've learned that moderate amounts of pain don't have to be a big problem. They come and go. I breathe, I stretch, I relax. I realize that I am aging, that I have these physical weaknesses, and that it's all part of having a body. And certainly I don't try to push myself.

Our culture and medical community will often try to tell us that we shouldn't have pain or that they can fix us, but that's not always true. The answer isn't always treatment. Sometimes it's just trying to keep our pain manageable, to live within our physical limitations—to lead a life that's not perfect, just livable.

Let's not pretend that real health issues can't have terribly negative consequences in our lives. But, as with difficult emotions, we can still have a high quality of life and quality of happiness despite physical challenges. It's not easy, though. We have to engage deeply and continually with these challenges.

REFLECTION **Physical Challenges**

Consider what physical challenges or difficulties you have in your life. How do you relate to these challenges? What emotions do they bring up for you? Can you accept your physical limitations? How can you work with or around them? ■

Mindful Movement

When I first started to go on Buddhist meditation retreats, I thought that walking meditation was there just to give your knees a break from sitting still in a cross-legged posture. These retreats were structured with continuous practice, except for meal times and sleep. You sat still for forty-five minutes, and you did slow walking for forty-five minutes. I found it difficult to hold the meditation position for that long, often struggling for the last third of the period just to remain seated. So walking meditation was a chance to get up and stretch my legs, go to the bathroom, and space out for a while.

As I went on longer and longer retreats over my first year of practice, I couldn't justify writing off such large chunks of time, and began to make more of an effort to connect with mindful walking. Soon my practice began to change.

Being in an upright posture and in movement allowed for an experience of the body that was new. While sitting allowed me to experience subtle sensations of energy in the body, walking began to feel like a dance. I felt the grace and flow of walking, the strange sensation of falling forward and catching myself with every step. I felt the complexity of the process of taking a step, all the muscles, bones, and ligaments involved in this seemingly simple activity. It was another case of waking up to life, seeing that there was more to life than I had previously assumed. The mindfulness practice is about discovering what life really is rather than what we think it is. It might seem as if we are looking only at the most rudimentary aspects of our existence, but what mindfulness shows us is that our existence is actually made of just a few things, in Buddhist terms: seeing, hearing, tasting, touching, smelling, and thinking. If we don't engage in these six sense experiences, we are missing life.

In some sense, this makes practice simple, because when we get lost or confused, we can just return to these six. With walking meditation, we are emphasizing "touching," all the sensations of movement. I found that as I practiced walking more carefully on retreat, when I was not on retreat, I also tended to be more mindful when I was walking. This was a great bonus, naturally bringing more mindfulness into my daily life.

As I was getting more and more immersed in meditation practice, I was also learning yoga. Many retreats included periods of yoga, and this was another valuable way to bring mindfulness into the body. Carefully moving into and holding a posture while remaining connected to the breath increased my concentration, which, again, increased my sensitivity to the nuances of sensation in the body. In addition, yoga has its own beneficial health effects as well as calming the mind and relaxing the body. The feeling of openness and release that comes with even a short session makes it even easier to be present. That's why many mainstream mindfulness programs now include yoga as part of their regimen.

The increased physical awareness I was developing on retreats had the further effect of making me more generally aware of my health, my diet, and physical condition. Unfortunately, a lot of these benefits were undermined by my continuing use of drugs and alcohol. I don't recall ever being particularly mindful of a hangover, other than wanting to find some aspirin. I did, at times, delude myself that I was doing mindful walking as I wove between the tables in a bar on the way to the stage, but I've since come to realize that any time you are drunk you have to make extra effort to stay upright, and that doesn't qualify as mindfulness.

My friend Greg Pergament, the author of *Chi Kung in Recovery*, likes to point out the dearth of information or discussion of health, exercise, and the body in Twelve Step literature. On retreats we have taught together, he invites people to connect with their bodies in a gentle and accessible way.

Buddhist mindfulness practices start with a focus on the body. While this isn't for the purpose of health particularly, beginning to pay attention to sensations in the body naturally makes you aware of how you are taking care of your body. There may be a tendency to think of addiction as mostly a mental problem, beyond the detox period, but many of us come to recovery with significant physical problems. Early Twelve Step literature suggested increasing sugar intake for newcomers, and I suspect that many people tend to overeat early in their recovery for a variety of reasons. Certainly some people come to recovery undernourished, as they have been punishing their bodies with excessive drugs and/or alcohol. And, of course, for many people, their relationship to food is a primary addiction: for an anorexic, eating more is healthy; for an overeater, it's deadly.

What also happens is that addicts replace their primary addiction with food. This becomes a source of comfort, pleasure, and numbing escape. If you are in a Twelve Step program that's not directly about food, you can easily slip into this behavior, and perhaps for a spell it's not unwise to just let yourself have some pleasure during that stressful time of early recovery. But at some point, if you don't start to taper back, then health can become a real issue.

In the next section, I'll talk about our relationship to food.

In Buddhist sanghas, many people engage in formal movement practices like yoga, chi kung, tai chi, and others. The beauty of such practices is their blending of mind and body, so that they increase awareness as they increase health and physical fitness. Some of these practices are very subtle in the ways they work. Chi kung, for instance, doesn't seem to be exercise at all sometimes, and yet when we finish a session we can often notice a big energetic shift. In addition, when we bring mindfulness to our exercise, we protect our bodies. This is one reason why listening to music as we work out can be risky. It tends to disconnect us from sensation and to allow us to push through pain in ways that can damage the body.

Obviously, the more spiritually oriented regimens are not the only ways to be mindful in movement. I've talked with many people who say that running or biking is meditative for them. Hikers connect with nature and beauty as they get their hearts pumping. Bringing together mindful attention with movement and exercise is one of the most enjoyable, healthy, and beautiful ways to blend our spiritual life and recovery directly into our lives.

REFLECTION **Mindful Movement**

What activities bring you in touch with your body? Are there physical activities you're already doing that you could bring mindfulness to in order to more consciously experience the subtle sensations of your body? Are there any practices or activities you could take up to increase that awareness? ▪

PRACTICE **Mindful Walking**

To practice formal mindful walking, find a flat, quiet area, either indoors or outdoors, where you can walk ten to thirty paces (indoors will typically be at the lower end of the scale). Start by standing still with the eyes closed for a few moments, just scanning the sensations in your body. Then open your eyes and very slowly lift your foot, feeling the sensation in the foot as it moves through space and gently lands again. As your weight shifts, move your attention to your other foot as it comes off the ground, moves through space, and comes down again. To stabilize the attention, you can make the soft mental notes "Lifting, moving, placing" as you perform these movements. Keep moving, not stopping between steps, until you reach the end of your chosen path. Stop, breathe, and turn around. Re-center yourself, and lift your foot and start back down the path. Do this exercise for five to twenty minutes.

As an alternative to paying attention to the sensations in your feet, you can pay attention more generally to the feeling of movement as you go through space. This can have the feeling of a subtle dance, moving rhythmically and gracefully as you walk. ▪

Mindful Eating

Many addicts ignore their diet while they are engaged in their addiction. Drugs and alcohol numb us and make us less sensitive to the effects of diet on our bodies, as well as often triggering cravings for sugar, fat, and carbohydrates. Of course, people whose drug of choice is food have a whole other challenge, which I'll address later.

For the alcoholic or drug addict who gets clean, sometimes food becomes a new addiction. With the pleasure of intoxication taken away, and the raw feelings of withdrawal and new recovery difficult to manage, eating unhealthy foods and overeating can be a way of numbing again. Some addicts simply never paid attention to diet and don't even know how to eat healthily.

As our bodies clean out and become more sensitive to what we put into them, as with so many things in recovery, we have to learn new ideas and change old behaviors. Bringing mindfulness into our eating is a good place to start.

On retreats, we're taught mindful eating as a meditation exercise in which we engage very slowly in every aspect of a meal: the cravings as we think about and approach the meal; the smells, sights, and tastes of the food; the changing sensations as we eat and approach (or pass) fullness; and the aftereffects of the meal, whether they are sleepiness, bloatedness, or comfort. Again, learning these practices on a retreat gives us great tools to carry over into our daily lives. Just as with walking meditation, which we also do very slowly on retreat, when we return to our daily lives, we probably won't have the inclination, much less the time, to linger over a forkful of brown rice, but we can carry over many of the concepts and teachings of mindful eating into our daily meals.

Being mindful of our relationship with food starts when we choose what we are going to eat. So even grocery shopping is brought into play. Stores and packaging are all set up to stimulate craving and encourage us to buy products, whether they are good for us or not, so as you walk down the aisle of the supermarket, it's wise to notice the cravings that come up and try to make wise decisions. Maybe those chips are your comfort food, or perhaps Ben & Jerry's just came out with a new flavor you've never tasted. It's not that we can't eat comfort food or desserts, but if we have any tendency to binge or overeat, we have to be careful. The researchers I've worked with who were developing a mindful-eating program say that normal eaters use food for comfort at times, but that unhealthy eaters overuse it. Only you can know what's right.

This brings us back to looking at our body's needs. An active teenage athlete can eat massive amounts of calories and not gain an ounce; a sedentary middle-aged office worker can't. And individual metabolisms vary so much that reading a package for the number of servings may only give us the vaguest sense of how much of the product we should eat.

This is where we draw on both our recovery program and our Buddhist practice. Recovery encourages us to be honest with ourselves. You might find it helpful to take a "food inventory," just exploring what healthy and unhealthy habits you have and reflecting on an appropriate diet *for you.* Our mindfulness practice helps us to penetrate deeper into our craving and our body sensations to see the driving energies and what our body really wants and needs.

PRACTICE   **Mindful Eating—The Raisin Exercise**

Begin by picking up one raisin. Smell the raisin. Feel the raisin in your fingers. Bring the raisin to your lips and touch it to them. Place the raisin on your tongue, but don't chew. Roll the raisin around on your tongue. Feel the saliva being released. Bite into the raisin and feel the skin break and the softness inside. Chew slowly, savoring the flavor on your tongue and taste in your mouth. Notice the raisin changing form until you need to swallow. As you swallow the raisin, feel it going down your throat and as far as you can follow it to your stomach.

Take a second raisin and repeat the exercise. Notice how the experience is different the second time. Take special note of the difference in flavor between when you are breathing in and when you are breathing out. Notice if your hunger is subsiding.

Before eating a third raisin, reflect on all the causes and conditions that brought the raisin to you: the earth, the sun, and the rain; the workers who pick the grapes and those who dry and package them; those who transport and those who sell the raisins. Reflect on the elaborate system of production and distribution that makes raisins so accessible to you, even if they are grown thousands of miles away. We are the beneficiaries of this system for which we might express gratitude and awe at the complexity of the interdependence we live in. ▪

PRACTICE   **Broadening Mindfulness of Eating**

Food is a preoccupation for many of us. Begin to notice the extent to which hunger and food are part of your life. Notice when hunger first arises between meals. Notice how that feels both physically and emotionally. Notice when the feeling of hunger transitions into a decision to eat something. As you are eating, notice how hunger decreases and fullness increases. Notice how full you need to be before you feel satisfied and stop eating.

Bring mindfulness into your food shopping as well. What is the basis for your food choices? Taste? Cost? Health? What draws you to certain foods and away from others? Could you make wiser choices in what you buy and what you eat? ▪

Enough Money

I've been amused by studies that show that across the financial spectrum, from the richest to the poorest, the typical response to how much more income or money would make someone happy is 10 percent. Each of us thinks that if we just had a little more money, we'd be set. What this tells me is that most of us don't actually feel that we don't have enough money, but rather that we *always want more*. This is how our minds work, and just what the Buddha was talking about. What's creating our suffering isn't the lack of money, but our wish for more, our desire. This is the second Noble Truth.

Let's not pretend, though, that grinding poverty doesn't make the elements of happiness I've defined difficult to achieve. It's tough to have integrity with the stresses and pressure of being poor; poverty puts a huge strain on families and marriages; it's rare that the kind of work the poor get is personally satisfying; and it's hard to spend time cultivating inner peace when we are struggling day-to-day to survive. What's clear is that a basic level of prosperity makes the potential for happiness much greater.

Given that baseline, though, as with our health, the key to happiness around money is our relationship to it. Here are a few negative ways that people relate to money:

- Greedy: Some people somewhat mindlessly want to accumulate money. While there may be things they want—a big house, fancy car, or exotic travel—none of those things really bring satisfaction, as there always seems to be a bigger house, fancier car, or more exotic locale to be acquired.

- Fearful: For many people, fear is a big issue around money. This is clearly part of greed, but doesn't necessarily result in the same behavior. Fear probably manifests more internally as worries and stress. It can also result in hoarding instead of using money in a way that supports happiness.

- Careless: Addicts are often irresponsible about money. They don't balance their bank accounts, let debt pile up, and spend impulsively.

- Anorexic: When we demonize money or consider it to be "unspiritual," we can cut ourselves off from something that is actually neutral, and something that, for a layperson in our society, is required for our survival. Living simply doesn't necessarily require poverty or deprivation. And, unfortunately, in our capitalist system, just surviving is somewhat expensive. To have access to health care, good food, and adequate housing and clothing costs quite a lot. If we reject money and try to live without it, we're going to have a hard time providing ourselves with these basics.

I'm sure there are other unskillful money habits, but the point is, if we are going to be happy with our financial situation, we need to first uncover any unwise, destructive, irresponsible, or counterproductive habits in our relationship to money. Once we see these habits clearly, we can make wiser choices, ones less driven by unconscious motives.

In the Buddhist world, I sometimes see a kind of post-hippie attitude about money—that it is somehow bad or unspiritual. One dharma-teacher friend realized as she got into her mid-thirties that she had a dysfunctional relationship to money, dismissing it as unimportant and an obstruction to her path—the anorexic relationship. Living in poverty and in debt, struggling to get by, she decided to address these problems and went to Debtors Anonymous. There, she was able to see that what she had justified as "spiritual" was really more immature and irresponsible. Now that she was getting older, planning marriage and motherhood, she realized she didn't want to live like that anymore. Eventually, she took the concrete steps to change both her relationship to money and her financial situation itself.

REFLECTION **Me and My Money**

Reflect on your relationship to money, on both the emotional and material levels. How do you feel about money? Does one of the "types" above apply to you? Or perhaps some other type? Does your financial situation need improvement? If so, what steps could you take to improve it? ■

SERIOUS UNHAPPINESS

My own work at "recovering joy" hasn't been simply a theoretical exercise or even just a "spiritual" project. I have struggled with depression and challenging moods since I was a teenager, and I don't think I've ever gone more than a few consecutive years without at least a few months of troubling moods. Mindfulness and the tools of recovery have been essential in navigating these challenges. They give me ways to engage with my moods and maintain a productive and rewarding life.

Moods and Mindfulness

Moods can seem so solid and permanent. When they stretch out for weeks or months, it can become frightening, and that fear itself can feed the negative emotions even further.

Painful moods and emotions can be confusing: "Am I just sad about a relationship breakup or am I falling into real depression?" "Do I need to change my life or change my attitude?" And, "How long have I been feeling this way?" As I said to my therapist recently when struggling with my moods, "It's not unreasonable to take a very negative attitude about much of what goes on in the world." Sometimes I can talk myself into a bad mood just by reading the newspaper. But when I find that I'm doing that every day, I have to begin to wonder if it's the world's fault or my own.

Fundamentally, then, one question is whether we are just in a difficult part of our lives situationally or whether there is an underlying mental state or condition that is feeding negativity into our thoughts and feelings. I'm not sure we can answer a question like that without the help of someone else, particularly a therapist. But a daily mindfulness practice, both as formal meditation and as a check-in throughout the day, can help us to detect if our thoughts are in a rut. Responding to virtually every situation with the same attitude—negativity, anxiety, anger, or some other distressing emotion—can be a big clue that there's some underlying unresolved issue or condition that needs care and attention.

Recently, having been stuck for quite some time in negative moods and depressive states, I went on a two-week silent retreat. Just three or four days into the retreat, I started to notice not so much that I felt happy per se, but that I was having increasingly positive thoughts. Part of the painful moods had been negative projections about the future, and now I started to notice pleasant fantasies appearing in my mind. Ordinarily, I would want to drop fantasies on a retreat, but under the circumstances, I was grateful and realized that they reflected a shift in my underlying mind states.

At the same time, I started to notice that I was enjoying the beauty of nature at the retreat center more than I had when I arrived. This was another shift. Before the retreat, I had been aware that I wasn't really enjoying life, and now I was—simply because I'd spent a few days meditating. I wasn't making an effort in meditation to be in a better mood; I was simply doing the mind training of building mindfulness and concentration. Clearly, that training was having a tremendously positive and healing effect on me. Even though I've been practicing for more than thirty years, I'd never had such stark proof of the beneficial effects of meditation. Coming out of the retreat, I felt as if I'd pushed the restart button in my mind, back to what felt like a normal state—one not clouded by sadness and negativity. It also gave me as much proof of the benefits of intensive meditation practice as I've ever had, and reinforced my faith in its healing power.

Another practice that has helped me is noticing the times when I'm *not* depressed, whether it's just walking down the street, enjoying a meal, sitting in a Twelve Step meeting, or any other moment in my day when I'm not stuck. This reminds me, then, that my moods aren't permanent or solid, despite the way they might feel. It also can show me which activities weaken the depression so I can focus on doing those things more often.

Life is often difficult. For addicts and alcoholics, it may be even more difficult than for the ordinary person. We need to bring effort and energy to maintaining or regaining pleasant moods.

For me, recovering joy isn't about ending painful moods forever. Instead, it has many dimensions: a focus on activities and attitudes that enrich my life; a long-term view that creates positive karma despite any transitory anxiety, grief, or despair; a short-term view that insists on doing what needs to be done no matter how I *feel* about it; doing energetically and emotionally uplifting activities; and accepting my own emotional "set point," as well as learning to hold moods in a spacious, forgiving, and compassionate way.

Know Yourself

One thing I know about myself is that I have to work at my mental health and stay engaged in healing my painful moods. I need to meditate in a serious way, work my program, exercise, rest, and do anything else I can think of to maintain better mental health. When I become passive, it's dangerous.

This is one of the real challenges of dealing with depressive moods, because those moods tend to make one passive. As you sink into such states, it becomes harder to engage, and a downward spiral can take over. Some kind of reboot becomes necessary. Sometimes a meditation retreat can do that for you. For an addict who can't quit, a treatment center might provide this. Sometimes medication might be needed.

I never wanted to go on antidepressants, but when, a decade or so ago, my wife told me that she didn't know if she could live with me much longer if I didn't, it was a wake-up call. I did what she asked, and I was able to break out of that difficult, sustained period of depression.

In the recovery world, there has been debate at times about using medication to deal with depression and anxiety. Some people believe that if you take drugs for your mood, you aren't really sober. Others feel that if something is prescribed and not abused, then there's nothing wrong with it. It seems that the latter view has become dominant, as many people in recovery struggle with depression or anxiety. What most find is that these drugs aren't really fun; they don't get you high, so they aren't addictive in any real sense.

Many addicts discover that once drugs and alcohol are completely cleared out of the system and mental clarity returns, crippling moods, mind states, and diagnoses radically subside and even completely disappear. However, occasionally just the opposite occurs: an underlying issue becomes apparent when the drugs and alcohol are no longer there to mask or mitigate it. It's important to realize that there are many severe mental and emotional conditions that don't respond to, or at least aren't manageable with, sobriety and meditation alone. While I've talked to people who found mindful breathing to be a great help in dealing with anxiety attacks, sometimes breathing isn't going to be enough to manage full-on panic. And while I've talked to schizophrenics about applying mindfulness to the voices in their heads, I don't see that as a sufficient treatment by any means. There have been plenty of times when my Twelve Step program and my Buddhist practice together have not been up to the task of cutting through my moods. That's why I've seen psychotherapists.

Although I've been in terrible states of sadness and despair, I haven't suffered an acute depressive episode or the extreme symptoms of clinical depression, which can include sleep disruption, loss of appetite, complete collapse of energy and motivation, and powerful suicidal thoughts. All of these symptoms and conditions require professional help.

Each of us needs to look at our emotional issues realistically and not idealize either Twelve Step programs or mindfulness practices. The Twelve Steps, while having a lot of potential for healing, are essentially about recovering from addiction, not necessarily cheering us up. Meanwhile, Buddhist meditation is at its core a practice to penetrate into the deepest truths and realities, not put you in a good mood or even reduce your stress.

I believe that we need to be "rigorously honest" about our condition and our challenges, and draw on whatever help we can find, whether that is the Twelve Steps, meditation, medication, therapy, or hospitalization. There are also many alternative-healing tools like amino acid therapy (see Julia Ross's *The Mood Cure*), Somatic Experiencing (see Peter Levine's *Waking the Tiger*), and many others. Therapies like Dialectical Behavioral Therapy (DBT) and Mindfulness-Based Cognitive Therapy (MBCT) bring Buddhist practices into a clinical setting, drawing on a combination of mindfulness and Western psychology to deal with stubborn emotional conditions.

Doing "joy work" is important and can complement other types of help we are getting; doing it alone may or may not be enough, depending on who we are and what our situation is at any given time. I view this book as one about lifting people from either a neutral or slightly low state to a more pleasant one in the short term, as well as creating the conditions for more stable and reliable mind states going forward.

There are no easy answers or snap fixes for serious unhappiness, although there's no doubt that engaging in a life of mindfulness and recovery gives us some of the best tools possible for finding happiness. I see both the Twelve Steps and Buddhist meditation as very useful and vital elements of creating a fulfilling life. I also think it's important that we stay open to every form of help we might need.

WHAT'S THE PLAN?

choosing to be happy

In the opening of this book, I mentioned *How We Choose to Be Happy*, by Rick Foster and Greg Hicks, a book one of my Buddhist teachers introduced me to over fifteen years ago. It is subtitled *The 9 Choices of Extremely Happy People—Their Secrets, Their Stories.* While the authors didn't have any explicit relationship to Buddhism, the things they identified as keys to happiness certainly fit with Buddhist principles. Many of these choices also sound like recovery principles.

As I developed the plan for my own book, I wanted to combine these nine choices with the topics of chapters 2 through 7 to create a road map for happiness. In a sense, then, this final chapter is an experiment. Much like my original work blending Buddhism and the Twelve Steps, what I'm doing here is taking the idea of the connection that I intuitively sense and following it to its logical conclusion. I think the results are pretty interesting. The reflections in this chapter include questions that have been part of my own process of seeking happiness. The definitions found under each choice are from Foster and Hicks.

I don't expect you to deeply explore every single reflection I've created. That would be daunting. But I hope you'll look them all over and

FOSTER AND HICKS'S NINE CHOICES

- Intention
- Accountability
- Identification
- Centrality
- Recasting
- Options
- Appreciation
- Giving
- Truthfulness

focus on the ones that call to you. I'm pretty sure you're going to find something here that resonates. Over time, you can come back and revisit this chapter and see if other elements of the plan could use some of your attention. In my experience, that's how personal growth works: my needs and focus change over time. Once again, there isn't a one-size-fits-all solution or a one-time fix that permanently answers all my needs or yours. Recovering joy is an ongoing process requiring engagement, willingness, and effort.

Intention

"The active desire and commitment to be happy, and the fully conscious decision to choose happiness over unhappiness."

Do you actually want to be happy?

It can be something of a shock to realize that we don't have a clearly defined goal of happiness. Maybe we think it's too trivial or that it's more important to give than to receive. I know that for me, the idea of happiness as a primary goal seemed somewhat superficial at one time. Perhaps deluded by romantic ideas of the tragic lives of artists and musicians, I couldn't make something like happiness my overt intention. At different times, I had goals like fame, wealth, love, or enlightenment, and I thought that all these things would *bring* happiness, but to simply find a way to happiness whatever the circumstances of my life didn't occur to me.

In the condition of codependence, we place other people's happiness before our own. While this idea of unselfishness can be admirable, when it gets to the level of enabling other's behavior or needing other people to be okay before we can feel okay, it moves into the area of dysfunction. Both Al-Anon, the Twelve Step program started by the wives of the founders of AA, and Co-Dependents Anonymous (CODA) try to help people to develop boundaries and limits around their caretaking so that they don't give up their own happiness for the sake of others. Fundamentally, these programs are founded in the realization that we are powerless over the behavior and feelings of other people, and that it's not our job to fix these people. Ultimately, we find that setting the intention for our own happiness takes nothing away from others, but, in fact, allows us to give more.

For an addict, a critical aspect of intention is learning to distinguish between the wish for happiness and the wish for pleasure. Finding authentic happiness can involve delayed gratification—or no gratification at all. The Buddha says that Right Intention includes the wish to let go, to be free from attachment, and the wish to be kind. To have the intention to be happy without clinging to hopes or dreams is the challenge. This involves seeing with wisdom: seeing that unskillful actions that might bring pleasure or temporary satisfaction have negative long-term karmic results.

This is the critical issue for someone trying to get clean and sober. There must be a willingness to give up the immediate pleasure or escape of intoxication for the long-term benefits of recovery. This willingness only comes when the consequences of getting loaded are fully accepted. The people who succeed in recovery are the people who really want to stop using, not necessarily the people who are the worst off. So intention is the key element of establishing recovery.

To establish the elements of happiness I've defined in this book, we need to bring the following clear intention:

- Intention to cultivate the conditions for happiness in our lives: we need to set happiness as a conscious goal in how we live our lives.

- Intention to act with integrity, in harmony with our values: we have to see the importance of integrity, how

153

lack of integrity causes disharmony and that integrity brings a sense of safety and well-being.

- Intention to create harmonious relationships: we have to learn to care for ourselves without being selfish, to balance our needs with the needs of others.

- Intention to find work that is both Right Livelihood and meaningful and joyful: we need to be open to possibilities and be willing to explore and learn about different forms of work. It's important to bring a creative attitude to finding work that will inspire us.

- Intention to cultivate our inner life and spiritual growth: we need to see the importance of mental training and cultivating nonreactivity. We can discover a radical inner peace, an open heart, and a world of mystery and beauty if we are willing to live mindfully and develop a spiritual practice.

- Intention to find joy in each day and each moment: we need to be willing to be present for our lives and engage with whatever is happening. We move away from putting off happiness and toward the potential in this moment.

REFLECTION **Intention for Happiness**

Reflect on your own wish for happiness:

- Is happiness a priority in your life?

- In what ways do other goals, views, or opinions conflict with the intention for happiness?

Set the intention to find ways to bring more happiness into your life. ■

REFLECTION   **Intention for Integrity**

- Review the "Walk the Talk" chapter (chapter 2) to clarify for yourself what your values are. Reflect on which elements of these values you are living up to and which elements you are coming up short on. Take some time to understand why there is a conflict between your values and your actions.

- If you are struggling with your recovery, make working your program the focus of your intention for integrity right now. Consider the suffering that your addiction causes, see that no satisfaction comes from that behavior, and resolve to change, setting up a specific plan.

- Make setting the intention to live by your values an aspect of your daily practice. This can be done at the end of your meditation period during a time of reflection. Think of particular issues you want to address, and come up with some ritual language like "May I refrain from harsh speech today" or "Just for today, may I avoid using intoxicants." Take in what you are saying to yourself; feel its importance. ∎

REFLECTION   **Intention for Relationships**

Consider your essential intentions for your relationships. Make a commitment to foster healthy, happy relationships.

- Reflect on the "People Who Need People" chapter (chapter 3) and clarify for yourself what you think will bring happiness in the various types of relationships in your life.

- Focus particularly on the relationships where there is conflict right now, and consider ways to alleviate that conflict. Take time to consider the causes of the conflicts, especially where you see repetitive patterns.

- If you are single and want to find a partner, reflect on what actions you can take to find someone, and make a commitment to follow through on those actions. ▪

REFLECTION **Intention for Work**

Consider your essential intentions in your work life. Make a commitment to find and maintain work that brings satisfaction as well as reasonable financial stability.

- Review the "Forty Hours of Happiness" chapter (chapter 4) and consider if your current work is satisfying to you and nourishes you in inner and outer ways.

- If your work isn't satisfying, reflect on what you'd rather do and the steps required to achieve that.

- Set the intention to pursue the work you want, one day at a time. ▪

REFLECTION **Intention for Inner Life and Spiritual Growth**

Consider your essential intentions in your inner life.

- Review the "It's an Inside Job" chapter (chapter 5) and consider ways your spiritual practice lives up to your wishes and ways that it doesn't.

- Consider what you are willing and able to do to deepen your spiritual practice. What types of meditation or other spiritual practices would you like to integrate into your life?

- Set your intention to work at the things that would bring more meaning and satisfaction to your inner life. ▪

REFLECTION **Intention for Fun**

Bringing joyful activities into our lives in a regular way is an essential part of recovering joy.

- Make the commitment to do activities from your "Identification" list (see the Reflection boxes in the "Identification" section, pages 164–166) on a regular, preferably daily, basis.

- Notice any inner obstructions to setting this intention and remember: if you don't have the intention to be happy, you probably won't be.

- What adjustments are you willing and able to make in your life in order to do more activities that bring you joy? ▪

Accountability

> "The choice to create the life you want to live, to assume full personal responsibility for your actions, thoughts, and feelings, and the emphatic refusal to blame others for your own unhappiness."

The Twelve Steps emphasize accountability. When we write a "searching and fearless moral inventory," we are holding ourselves accountable for the way our lives have unfolded. Making direct amends lets others know we take responsibility for our actions.

When we become accountable, we are no longer victims. We see how much power we actually have, and we begin to use it. Of course, we can't control everything, but if we are honest, we see how much we can affect our own happiness: "Am I really doing what I can to create happiness in my life?" "Do I expect others to solve my problems or provide me with comfort and joy?" "Have I taken the actions that will result in contentment?"

It's easy to blame others, society, or our upbringing for our difficulties, and often enough, these things do create great challenges in our lives. But the problem with blaming these people, places, and things is that it undercuts our own potential to create our own happiness.

Accountability was something I avoided before I got sober. I don't know how much I blamed others for my problems, but I was certainly fatalistic. If things didn't work out, they were "just not meant to be." While I convinced myself that this was just "letting go," it was really more about fear, lack of self-confidence, and laziness. Achieving anything in the world seemed bewildering to me. I really couldn't understand how people did things like make money, get married, raise kids, or even find happiness. I felt doomed to live the life I lived, my only hope that some magical event like being "discovered" as a musician or getting "enlightened" as a meditator would save me. But fundamentally, I was unwilling to do the work involved to get what I wanted. And somehow I'd convinced myself that it wasn't work that brought results, but luck. This view absolved me of responsibility. Unfortunately, it was also what doomed me.

Much, if not all, of what I've accomplished in recovery has to do with a shift in this attitude. Starting with Step Four, I began to learn about accountability. And working with a wise and compassionate sponsor helped me learn how to work toward long- and short-term goals. The idea of showing up, taking one simple step each day, became my guiding principle. This principle allowed me to go back to school and get two degrees over seven years; it allowed me to write books, and it's allowed me to live with challenges and struggles over these decades without running away or giving up.

Accountability means we are looking at our side of the street. We become willing, as Steps Four through Nine (especially Nine) teach us, to be wrong and to see our mistakes. If we don't see our mistakes, we have no chance to correct them or to grow. If we are blaming others, we learn nothing. This doesn't mean that we are to blame for everything that goes wrong in our lives, just that we are trying to be very clear about what we can and can't do about it.

Accountability also means taking responsibility for our feelings. Some years ago, a couples counselor pointed out to me the fallacy of the statement "You made me feel . . ." No one can make me feel something.

Their actions can trigger my responses, but they didn't create the feeling. When I see that my feelings come from inside me, and are the results of my past experiences, actions, conditioning, and a whole range of factors, then I can respond differently to them. Mindfulness allows me to hold my feelings with much more space, wisdom, and compassion. I may still respond to how someone treats me, but not with blame.

To establish the elements of happiness I've defined in this book, we need to apply accountability in the following ways:

- We hold ourselves accountable for our integrity, for acting in harmony with our values; we don't make excuses or cut corners in our behavior.

- We hold ourselves accountable for creating harmonious relationships. We don't blame others or expect them to act on our behest. We take responsibility for the ways we hurt people and move to heal our side of the street, as well as make the effort to bring love, compassion, and forgiveness to others.

- We take accountability for finding work that is both Right Livelihood and meaningful and joyful. We take responsibility for finding work that is truly fulfilling, not allowing ourselves to get trapped in meaningless or destructive employment.

- We take accountability for our inner peace and open heart, making the time and space for our inner life and spiritual practice. We don't put off inner work or discount its importance. We don't blame others or circumstances for our lack of peace.

- We hold ourselves accountable for taking care of our health to the extent possible. We watch our diet, exercise regularly, and seek medical help for any health issues.

- We hold ourselves accountable for our financial circumstances. We are responsible with money and take the actions that allow us to make an amount of money that provides at least for our needs.

- We hold ourselves accountable for finding joy in each day and each moment. We recognize that our joy is our responsibility, not that of anyone or anything else. We see that even in the most trying times, we can discover a kernel of joy or meaning.

REFLECTION **Accountability for Integrity**

Integrity is all about accountability.

- Reflect on your our motives and actions to make sure they are in alignment with your values.

- Reflect on any changes in your lifestyle or habitual behaviors that would align you more with your values. Take action to align your actions with your values.

- If you are struggling with your recovery, reflect on the part you play in your own addiction, as well as look for the ways that you blame others for your problems. ▪

REFLECTION **Accountability in Relationships**

Look at how you blame other people for your dissatisfaction or unhappiness. Consider what power you have to change your life.

- Reflect on ways you blame others for your actions, feelings, and unhappiness.

- Make a commitment to be accountable to others. ▪

REFLECTION **Accountability in Work**

How many of us are unhappy in our jobs? Do we accept responsibility for that? Are we willing to either accept the limits of what our job has to offer or take the risks involved in change?

- Reflect on your relationship to your work. If you aren't satisfied, consider the alternatives and make a plan for change, whether it's a change in employment or a change in attitude. ▪

REFLECTION **Accountability for Inner Life and Spiritual Growth**

Many people say they want to increase their spiritual practice but struggle to carry through on that desire.

- Make a commitment to yourself to show up for your own spiritual life, setting aside time daily for meditation and reflection, and periodically for retreat.

- Notice the resistance and excuses you make, and continue to show up anyway. ▪

REFLECTION **Accountability for Fun**

Many of us put off doing things that aren't economically productive or fulfill some social or perceived responsibility.

- Recognize that you are responsible for finding joy in your life. Notice when you want to blame work, family, or other obligations for your lack of relaxing or playful activities.

- Once you've done the "Identification" and "Centrality" Reflections/exercises (see pages 164–166 and 167–168), note how it is up to you to make the daily choice to take time for yourself. ▪

REFLECTION Accountability for Health

Much of our health is out of our hands due to genetics, aging, and life's blows. However, we can have a big impact through diet, exercise, rest, and the ways we deal with stress.

- Acknowledge the ways you don't take care of your health and the ways you do.

- Review the specifics of diet, exercise, rest, and stress, and take responsibility for making changes that will improve your health.

- Do you seek medical help when you have problems or do you avoid doctors or ignore problems until they get worse? ■

REFLECTION Accountability with Money

- Look at the "Me and My Money" Reflection in the "Health and Wealth" chapter (chapter 7), and consider your relationship with money.

- Do you give your financial needs enough consideration? If your finances are problematic, consider whether that is due to some behavior or attitude on your part or whether your skills and education limit you. Perhaps the economy itself is the problem, or maybe you live in an area where your talents aren't in demand. What can you do to improve any deficit?

Identification

"The ongoing process of looking deeply within yourself to assess what makes you uniquely happy, apart from what you're told by others should make you happy."

As an addict, I had very limited ideas of what I liked to do: I didn't want a day job, so I was limited to being a musician; I liked to stay stoned, so I smoked pot daily; I rebelled against mainstream culture, so I lived in poverty; I dropped out of school, so I had very few options in life; I didn't want responsibilities, so I stayed single and childless.

Over time, I learned that many of these choices failed to make me happy, and I spent the first dozen years of my recovery doing what I could to reverse them. I surrendered to having a day job and realized the rewards; I discovered the joy of sobriety, living clean and healthy; I realized that my rebelliousness was mostly an immature reaction to facing the responsibilities of adulthood, which I now found satisfying to fulfill; and I went back to school and discovered a long-nascent love of learning and thinking. I found that as I matured in all these ways, responsibility wasn't so onerous, and I got married and became a father, two things that brought me tremendous joy and comfort.

Addiction and its attendant immaturity put enormous limitations on our lives. Without the clarity of recovery, it's easy to stay stuck in a cycle of fear and negativity that forces us to live a circumscribed existence, bound by the life-denying rules of addiction. Without engaging a recovery path, it was virtually impossible for me to address the depth and breadth of crippling views and behaviors that had kept true happiness out of my reach for so many years.

In shedding the limitations that addiction puts on us, we can realize that opportunities for happiness are all around us. In recovery, we can remember what makes us truly happy.

To establish the elements of happiness I've defined in this book, we need to identify these things:

- Our values.

- What is important to us in our relationships, as well as identifying the specific people who are important to us. When we come to understand the fruitlessness of a self-centered, pleasure-seeking life, we come to value new and different ways of connecting with people.

163

- Work that is both Right Livelihood and meaningful and joyful: As our self-image opens up, new possibilities of livelihood appear as well. If we don't believe the old limitations of who we think we are, what we think we can do, and what we might enjoy, a world of options is available.

- Our spiritual inspiration: There are many paths and practices. Exploring the paths and forms of inner work is one of the joys of recovery.

- Joy in each day and each moment: When we open ourselves up, we discover that the world is full of opportunities for joy. When we are no longer bound to addictive substances as the source of pleasure, we find multifold attractions right before us.

Now we are going into the heart of the plan. You'll want to spend plenty of time with the following Reflections, to identify your unique elements of happiness.

REFLECTION **Identifying Your Values**

Reflect on the values that, when you live in harmony with them, bring you happiness.

- What is truly important to you?

- How do you want to live?

- Are all of your values truly yours? Are you holding on to any values simply because society or other people have conditioned you to believe they are important? If so, are those values that contribute to your happiness?

- Either write down or make very clear to yourself what your own values are. ■

REFLECTION **Identifying Joy in Relationships**

Our lives are filled with relationships with family, partner, friends, colleagues, and more.

- Who are the people who really feed you, and who are those who drain you?

- What brings you happiness in your intimate relationships?

- What kind of support, care, treatment, training, or teachings do you need from a sponsor, therapist, or spiritual teacher? ■

REFLECTION **Identifying Joy in Work**

- What aspects of your profession or work do you enjoy? What aspects do you not enjoy?

- What can you change about your work situation that would allow you to do your work with joy? ■

REFLECTION **Identifying Your Spirituality**

There are many spiritual paths and various pressures to follow them.

- Reflect on your own beliefs and spiritual practices, getting clear about what brings you peace and a sense of connection.

- What motivates your spiritual practice and beliefs? Are you guided by your own heart and intuition, or by outside pressures such as society, family, or religious tradition? Is your path influenced by fear or superstition?

- Do your spiritual path and practices contribute to your happiness? ■

REFLECTION **Identifying Fun**

Make a list of every nonproductive activity you can think of that
makes you happy, from the trivial to the grand. Remember what
made you happy as a child. Don't leave out anything, no matter
how you think it makes you look.

- What do you already do for fun?

- What other activities could you do for fun? ▪

Centrality

> "The nonnegotiable insistence on making that which
> creates happiness central in your life."

This marks the point of bringing our intention into reality, putting
our plan into action. It's not enough to think about happiness; we also
have to act on it.

As I became engaged in this work, having identified and made a
list of the things that made me happy, I wanted to follow through. It
was suggested in the "Awakening Joy" course that if you were serious
about happiness that you do *something* from your list every day. I was
already doing some of these things, like meditating, playing catch with
my daughter, and taking walks. That's also when I decided to follow
the impulse to take up golf.

Recovering joy is about more than having fun, though. Making joy
or happiness central in our lives is a real commitment, and often requires
some letting go. I talk to many people who struggle with overwork, and
the demands of a corporate environment. When you have bills to pay and a
family to support, how are you supposed to make happiness central in your
life? Facing this kind of question is really key to this plan. It might be easy
to identify some playful activity you'd like to add to your life, but when so
much time is devoted to work, finding the joy there seems to be required.

Many people probably could be happier in their work, but
there's no doubt that this takes some creativity, some effort, and

maybe some letting go. Some of the things that may be necessary might be returning to school, moving to another area, or changing your lifestyle. It might take several years to execute a plan, but if we really want to change, to find the happiness that eludes us in our work, then we need to think in these ways. When I finished grad school, I attended a few career-transition workshops and was surprised by the number of lawyers who were participating. Law school is one of those options that many people choose based not on what will make them happy but on future earnings, founded in the delusion that making a lot of money will solve life's problems and somehow bring happiness—despite all evidence to the contrary. Certainly, some people are well suited to the rigors of the legal profession, but I'm pretty sure that what makes them happy as lawyers isn't their billing rate, but rather the intellectual engagement of solving problems and perhaps the wish to engage in bringing fairness or justice to people.

Making and keeping happiness central to our lives sometimes requires discipline, and some people have trouble with that. Meditation is one of the things I identified as making me happy. I remember someone asking me how I managed to go on a two-week retreat when I had a job and family. My response: "I plan it." Usually many months in advance, I create the circumstances necessary to take that time. I talk to my wife and daughter, and (when I had a job) discuss taking time off (sometimes unpaid) with my boss. I save money beforehand to cover the costs and the loss of income. These are the things we do when we want something, when we know how important something is to our happiness.

Along with identification, centrality holds the keys to this plan for happiness. We need to see what makes us happy, and then we need to do those things. Simple as that—but not so easy.

REFLECTION Centrality of Integrity

It's easy for us to cut corners or makes rationalizations about honesty and integrity. However, if we want to find peace and ease within ourselves, we need to stay true to our values.

- Commit to living on a daily basis the values you named in the "Identifying Your Values" Reflection (page 164). Bring these values into every aspect of your life, from the personal to the professional. ■

REFLECTION **Centrality of Relationships**

Do you spend time with the people you really love? How do you treat them? How do you treat the people who aren't as important to you? ■

REFLECTION **Centrality of Satisfying Work**

Work takes up a great deal of our lives, and if we can't enjoy it, we are writing off that piece of our lives.

- Commit to finding work that inspires you or brings meaning to your life. If you can't find such work, commit to getting the most happiness out of the work you do have.

- What would it take for you to engage yourself fully in your chosen work every day? ■

REFLECTION **Centrality of Inner Life and Spiritual Growth**

Having identified what has meaning and value for you in your inner spiritual life, commit to a daily practice. ■

REFLECTION **Centrality of Fun**

Having identified the playful activities that bring you joy, commit to doing at least two of these activities every day. ■

Recasting

> "The choice to convert problems into opportunities
> and challenges, and to transform trauma into
> something meaningful, important, and a source
> of emotional energy."

This choice makes me think of the "Promises" from the AA Big Book that say, "We will not regret the past, nor wish to shut the door on it. . . . We will come to see how our experience can benefit others." When you've been through the trauma of addiction, you've got to do something with all of that history. While in some ways we just want to move on (after we've made amends), finding other ways to hold and respond to the past is more helpful.

I'm always so moved when people who've lost a child to a disease decide to devote their lives to finding a cure. We hear many stories like this, and it reflects the epitome of "recasting." But each of us has problems, failures, and tragedies, and finding a way to convert them to something positive is critical to happiness. Otherwise, we are either trying to suppress or deny these wounds or indulging in guilt, regret, and despair.

Certainly, overcoming an addiction and helping others who suffer is one of the obvious ways that we can recast the damage of our past. Step Twelve says that once we've achieved the "spiritual awakening" of the Steps, we should "carry this message" to other addicts. This allows us to use the actual structure of the Steps to recast our experience as something useful. Besides the many people who do service like this for free, treatment centers are largely staffed by people who were once addicts themselves.

This step helps us to get past limiting ideas of right and wrong, good and bad, and especially success and failure. Over a lifetime, we can often look back and see that what we thought was a bad thing turned out to have an unforeseen value. Many people in recovery have this view. Certainly, I can see that without the Twelve Steps and all I've learned in recovery programs, my life would be very different. I might have limped along or gotten by without really facing the challenges that admitting my problem with drugs and alcohol forced me to tackle. When I go into a treatment center to teach mindfulness or someone thanks me for my work, it's easy to see that the "failure" of alcoholism and drug addiction has led to some of my greatest "success."

REFLECTION   **Recasting Failure**

- Reflect first on your addiction and recovery and all that you have gained and contributed to the world through recovery from addiction. Had you never been an addict, you could never have done these things.

- Now reflect on the big mistakes and failures of your life: Have you been able to learn and grow from these failures? If not, can you now consider ways to view these experiences differently? What lessons have you learned? What wisdom has been gained? Has compassion or understanding grown? Have you ever been able to share with someone one of your failures in a way that might have helped them? ■

Options

> "The decision to approach life by creating multiple scenarios, to be open to new possibilities and to adopt a flexible approach to life's journey."

For addicts, there are no options. That's what addiction is: the compulsion to do the same thing over and over. It makes life simple—there are no decisions to make, just like in prison.

One recovery cliché is "We have choices today." My friend and dharma teacher Sandra Weinberg tells us, "Desire narrows our awareness till we see only what we crave; mindfulness helps us see other possibilities."

Options were one of the biggest doorways to freedom I found in recovery. As I've told you, I had created many limitations in my life in terms of work, relationships, spirituality, and worldview. I was stuck in so many ways that I couldn't even see. It reminds me of the line from the Eagles' song "Hotel California": "We are all prisoners here, of our own device." And it's remarkable how we believe that others created this self-imposed cage, that somehow we are victims. This is the delusion of addiction.

It took me some time to break out of these shackles in early recovery. At first, I just kept doing what I'd been doing, playing music in clubs and hoping for a break into the business, something that would get me out of the small-time club world. But a year in, as I started to really engage the program and the Steps, I began to ask myself questions. If I wasn't going to be a rock star, was there something else I could do? This was the inquiry that led me down the path I described in the chapter "Forty Hours of Happiness": trying out working at a record company. When I look back on those days, I take some joy in the choices I made, choices that weren't easy for me and that took some humility. (I know, bragging about humility is an oxymoron.) At first, I thought I'd give up my rock-star dream to become a rock-star producer. When that didn't pan out, falling back on simply learning to type and taking whatever opportunities came from that basic skill set in motion an amazing (to me) karmic unfolding that led straight to this book. But it starts with my willingness at three years sober to look at my options, to not stay stuck in one vision of how my life was supposed to play out. I'd finally seen the failure of my own fantasies and prejudices, the limited vision of who and what I could be.

I've needed options throughout my recovery. When I decided to go back to school, I thought I'd become a psychologist. This seemed logical based on my life experience. Plus, many dharma teachers and people in recovery were therapists, so it seemed like a safe option. At the end of my first semester of college, my English teacher suggested I explore writing as a career. Because I wanted to get away from the arts, I at first scoffed at the idea. But I was also learning to listen to the wisdom of others, and so took up creative writing. At the same time, I was researching careers for therapists and discovered how competitive that field was. The option of writing started to look more feasible, especially as I found myself enjoying those classes more and more.

Eventually, though, I fell back into my typical myopic approach, deciding I was going to be a novelist. An agent actually picked up my first novel when I was still an undergraduate, and my dreams continued to expand. Though it didn't get published, it got me into grad school where I wrote another novel. When, after two years of graduate school, I hadn't published either novel or sold any of the screenplays I'd started writing, I graduated a failure. At least, that's how I felt.

At that point, though, I fell back on the fact that I did have some skills. Typing! Data entry!

With great humility (and not a little desperation), I took a temp job doing data entry with a contractor for the Pacific Gas and Electric Company. On the first day of work, I sat with forty other temps entering data from piles of sheets about potentially defective wall heaters that the company had installed as part of a government program. Being the serious reader I was, I immediately started catching errors on the sheets that had been filled out by hand by inspectors. Each time I'd call to the manager, he'd come over to my workstation. "Good catch," he'd say, and we'd try to straighten out the problem.

By the end of the week, half the people were gone from the project, and I had been promoted. A month later, just a few of us were left, and I'd become the right-hand assistant to the manager.

Data entry is considered a very low-rung job, and yet I found it interesting. It became clear to me why so much computer data is flawed: because data entry is a low-rung job done by people without a lot of reading and writing, or, for that matter, logic, skills. My greatest triumph in the job was one day finding an address that appeared to be simply nonsense characters that someone had randomly hit on a keyboard. Something about the characters got my attention, and I realized that the person had had their hand positioned one space to the side on the keyboard. I was able to decipher the address that they meant to key in.

Still, data entry didn't seem like a good long-term career fit, so that first year out of grad school, I kept looking in the paper (where jobs were still listed back in 1996) for jobs with the word "writer" in their title. Eventually, I came upon "technical writer," and began to do some research. In fact, my data-entry job had morphed into a certain amount of user-manual writing, and I began to think that I might be able to get one of these tech-writer jobs.

At the time, the early dot-com revolution, writers were at a premium in the tech world, and I managed to talk my way into an entry-level technical-writer position, which was the best-paying job I'd ever had. It was the beginning of a twelve-year career.

Did I want to be a technical writer? No way. Did I think I had more to offer the world than that? Sure I did. But nobody was publishing my novels, in the same way that nobody had recorded my songs. I could have decided it was "novelist or bust," but I'd done that as a musician, and I didn't want to repeat that life. Unlike when I was a musician, I didn't feel that my happiness depended on writing novels. I didn't feel that my self-esteem was grounded in having my name on a book jacket. I needed to make a living, I wanted to be comfortable, and I'd learned something about being flexible, about acceptance, and about where happiness actually came from: inside.

Of course, options apply to the other aspects of happiness as well. Early in recovery, I realized that my decision-making around relationships didn't work, and I became open to new ways of operating that my sponsor recommended. I've already talked about discovering golf as an option for fun. Our spiritual lives can draw on many possibilities as well. All of this, and more, applies to the choice of options.

Options are important in our daily lives as well, in the many ways we might get stymied trying to do something or solve a problem. Having a sense of openness and possibility, rather than always setting ourselves just one path, makes our lives so much more easeful.

The choice to have options is connected to Step Three, turning our will and our lives over. This pivotal Step in the Twelve Step process teaches us to not cling so tightly to how we think things should be and to accept the results of our actions. Implicit here is the idea that there are many ways that things can play out satisfactorily in our lives. Addiction is an attempt to control our feelings, a resistance to change and the mutability of life. It fails because feelings can't be controlled, change is inevitable, and coming into harmony with those realities, not trying to resist them, is the way to happiness.

Connecting with options is a creative act. Creativity is opening the mind to possibilities, allowing new ideas and views to appear. When we're stuck on one track, we can't see the possibilities. If we're going to see those possibilities, we have to let go. For many of us, it takes some kind of disaster or collapse in our lives—losing a job, the death of a loved one, getting arrested for drunk driving—to force us to question our choices. Is there another way? As addicts, we spend years building a single-pointed worldview and belief system, especially regarding our beliefs about ourselves. Until we realize that these limitations are largely our own construction, we won't be able to discover any options in our lives.

REFLECTION   **Options in Relationships**

- In what ways can you foster and nurture relationships with those people who feed and support your happiness?

- If there are classes of relationship you *don't* have, like intimate or community or friendly, what options do you have for finding and developing such relationships?

- If you are in a difficult relationship with someone—personal, professional, or otherwise—what changes could you make to the dynamic between you? What options besides conflict or separation can you find? ∎

REFLECTION   **Options in Work**

- If you aren't happy or satisfied with your career, reflect on the ways you could be limiting possibilities in your career.

- Take a skills inventory of some kind, whether formal or informal, and start to broaden your ideas of career paths.

- Which careers would your skills and interests be useful for besides the one you are currently in?

- How would you go about changing careers? Start at the beginning. You don't have to figure it out all at once. ▪

REFLECTION **Options in Spiritual Practice**

- What options have you explored in spiritual practice?

- Do you make time for spiritual practice? If not, how could you make more time for it?

- If you're in a rut with practice, what steps could you take to break out of it? ▪

REFLECTION **Options for Fun**

- In what ways do you limit your options for fun?

- What new ways of having fun are you willing to try? ▪

Appreciation

"The choice to appreciate deeply your life and the people in it and to stay present by turning each experience into something precious."

Appreciation is perhaps the choice most directly related to mindfulness. I've described returning to my hometown after my first meditation retreat. It was like waking up from a long sleep. All of a sudden, I saw everything in a new light—the beautiful old houses, the tree-lined streets, the river and the mountains.

When we're caught inside our heads, we miss so much of life. In our effort to figure everything out—to plan, remember, process, calculate, and criticize—what's actually happening goes by with no recognition. It's hard pulling ourselves out of that place where we live so much of the time. It feels safe in there, and it can be scary to let that all go and just be, just see, hear, feel. But that's life, and if we want to get the most out of life, we have to pay attention.

Sometimes—oftentimes—all it takes to appreciate the moment is to stop all the thinking and engage the present. What is there to appreciate right now? A person? Nature? Your work?

In my model, we see we can appreciate our integrity, our relationships, our work, our inner life, and our opportunities for play.

This practice encourages us to be present for life just as it is. Nonjudgmental awareness allows us to appreciate everything, even things that we don't like. Perhaps this doesn't always bring joy, but at least it brings acceptance. If we are only able to appreciate pleasant or positive things, we miss a lot of opportunities. Certainly when someone says they are a "grateful alcoholic" or addict, they are expressing this appreciation for something that, while it probably created a lot of pain and chaos in their lives, eventually led them to the awakening of recovery. Pain and challenges in our lives are the biggest motivators to change, so our ultimate relationship to them can quite naturally become appreciation.

REFLECTION **Appreciation of Integrity**

Reflect on your own integrity in recovery, perhaps in comparison to your earlier life of addiction. See how your integrity benefits you and others, and take joy in that. ▪

REFLECTION **Appreciation of Relationships**

- Reflect on your relationships, taking joy in the people you love and who love you.

- During your meditation practice, offer lovingkindness and compassion to those you care about. ■

REFLECTION **Appreciation of Work**

If you are employed, reflect on the benefits you receive from your work and take joy in them:

- Financial support

- Contributing to the world

- Opportunity to be of service

- Opportunity to engage intellectually and creatively ■

REFLECTION **Appreciation of Inner Life**

Reflect on the preciousness of the spiritual teachings you have been given and take joy in them. ■

REFLECTION **Appreciation of Fun**

Reflect on the joyful activities you are able to take part in. ■

REFLECTION **Appreciation of Difficulties**

Reflect on what you have learned and gained from the challenges you have faced in your life. ■

Giving

"The choice to share yourself with friends and community and to give to the world at large without the expectation of a 'return.'"

Generosity and service are vital aspects of both the Buddhist teachings and Twelve Step program. When we focus on the welfare of others, we both get out of ourselves and bring good to the world.

When the Buddha attained his enlightenment, he realized there was nothing else to do for himself. Perhaps, too, having seen through the illusion of self, he realized that trying to satisfy an illusion was pointless. He saw that there was nothing else to do but try to help others, to teach them what he had learned so that they could have the same freedom he had attained. He spent the next forty-five years of his life walking the dusty roads of North India offering his teachings.

Step Twelve suggests that once we have worked the rest of the Steps, "having had a spiritual awakening," we do the same thing as the Buddha, though, of course, on a more modest scale: "to carry this message" to those who still suffer from addiction. Again, this points to two fundamental spiritual axioms: one, that when we help others we have no time to worry about ourselves, which relieves us of self-obsession; and two, that ultimately we'll never satisfy our endless longings, so it's pointless to try.

Unfortunately, all of this kindness, service, and generosity may not be so instinctive for an addict—it certainly wasn't for me. But as my sponsor took me through the Steps, I just kind of did the next thing he suggested. When I got to Step Twelve, he said I should take some service commitments at meetings and start to sponsor others. Sponsoring at this stage seemed premature, but I did sign up to sweep a meeting room after the weekly gathering. Quickly, I learned the magic of service.

While I'd been meeting people and getting more comfortable as a Twelve Step member, when I started to do service, I was thrown into the middle of the community. Now my name was mentioned at the end of every meeting—"And thanks to Kevin for cleaning"—and I met all the other service people. Instead of just hanging around, now I was part of the organization (I use the term loosely). I felt completely different and saw that I was looked upon differently. People appreciate service, and they know that it reflects a deeper commitment than just coming to a meeting, or in the Buddhist world, to a class or retreat. It's understood that people who give really *get it.* Sweeping the floors was seen as reflecting humility.

Many people know that helping others, being of service, or giving of yourself feels good, but I didn't. I'd really never learned the joy of giving. The simple answer for that was, I was selfish.

Before I got sober, on my first few meditation retreats I was given the option of helping out in the kitchen or in various housekeeping tasks. I passed. "That's for suckers," I thought. "I'm here to meditate and get enlightened, not do dishes." Clearly, I didn't get it.

I'm still not the most generous person, but at least service and giving are in my vocabulary today. Our lives offer so many opportunities for giving, from helping someone on the street, to caring for an aging parent or young child, to bringing an attitude of service to our work life.

Like many other aspects of the spiritual life, giving also has its shadow. What we call codependence is one shadow of service and generosity. When we feel that we can't do enough or that the only way we will be loved is if we take care of others' needs before our own, then we have gone too far. We can only know for ourselves whether we are truly giving of ourselves or seeking love by giving ourselves away.

REFLECTION   **Giving as a Value**

Is generosity or giving one of your values? If so, how are you living that value? If not, is it a value worth considering adding to your life? ▪

REFLECTION   **Giving in Relationships**

- Reflect on the joy you get from giving love, care, and support to friends, family, intimates, colleagues, and others.

- Could you give more in your relationships? ▪

REFLECTION **Giving in Work**

Reflect on the joy you get from being of service in your work. Be specific in who it is that is served by your work. Can you take that knowledge in with joy? ▪

REFLECTION **Giving as Spiritual Practice**

Reflect on the joy of generosity and think about how you can bring more generosity into your life, either through material giving or service. ▪

REFLECTION **Joy in Giving**

- What forms of giving bring you special joy?

- What are you longing to give? ▪

REFLECTION **Unhealthy Giving**

If you have the tendency to give yourself away, either with time, care, or resources, reflect on the motivation behind that habit. If you aren't in a program, consider Al-Anon or CODA. ▪

Truthfulness

> "The choice to be honest with yourself and others in an accountable manner by not allowing societal, corporate, or family demands to violate your internal contract."

I don't know if the kind of truthfulness I relate to is what Foster and Hicks meant, but for me, being open and honest is a critical part of my life, both in recovery and in the Dharma. Right Speech, as I talked about in chapter 2, is central to Buddhist teachings and part of the Eightfold Path.

I learned about being truthful with myself when I worked Steps Four through Nine. Up to then, I'd mostly felt guilt, shame, and defensiveness about my mistakes and failings. Something shifted, though, as I wrote my inventory and shared it, and finally made amends. At the same time, I'd begun sharing at meetings, and the overall effect was powerful.

I think even before I did that work, just hearing others sharing in meetings had a big impact. It amazed me to hear people talk about themselves in such honest and revealing ways. Much of what I heard reminded me of my own mistakes and failings, so that by the time I got to Step Four, I already felt less isolated and unique in what I was writing about in my inventory.

It's still somewhat amazing to me the shift that happened over those months of writing and sharing. By the time I finished my amends process, I think my relationship to my ego had had a profound shift. This is what I think they mean by a "spiritual awakening." This isn't to say that I no longer had an ego or that there haven't been episodes of defensiveness, guilt, shame, or regret since then, but before this process I was completely defended and unwilling to look at my negative qualities in any kind of honest way. Now the phrases "I was wrong" and "I made a mistake" became part of my vocabulary. This has made life so much simpler.

When I began to teach dharma and tried to figure out how to give a talk, at first I tried to be like some of my teachers, giving a wise, detached version of the Dharma. Soon, though, this started to feel like a tight suit of clothes—restrictive and uncomfortable—and not me. At times, I'd write out a talk, then start to digress and discover I couldn't find my way back to the text. Eventually, I found that this effort to project an image just wasn't workable for me, and I began to bring more of my experience and personality into my teaching. I don't know whether that made me a better teacher, but it did make the experience better for me. I'm sure there are those who don't appreciate my style, in the same way there are surely people who don't appreciate my books, but there's no point trying to satisfy everyone as long as what I'm doing is useful for some.

In any case, as this shift started, I realized that it was my experience sharing truthfully in Twelve Step meetings that was really informing my teaching style. It felt freeing to just be myself, and in fact, this became my guiding principle in teaching: be yourself.

Over the years, I decided that instead of presenting an ideal to people, I'd rather present a human being, with all his failings and quirks. I've actually found it painful at times when I compared myself to the image I saw in some of my teachers, so I've thought that if people could see a teacher as like them, just another person struggling on the path, they might feel less of the pain of that projection.

Truthfulness is key to all the elements of happiness: it is central to integrity, absolutely necessary to healthy and happy relationships, critical in work if we want to be of service, and integral to inner work.

REFLECTION **Truthfulness in Relationships**

Reflect on your truthfulness in your relationships. Are you truly honest or are there ways in which you skirt the truth for your own benefit or out of fear? ■

REFLECTION **Truthfulness in Work**

Reflect on your truthfulness in your work. Are you truly honest or are there ways in which you skirt the truth for your own benefit or out of fear? ■

REFLECTION **Truthfulness Inside**

- How truthful are you with yourself?

- Are there any issues or areas of your life where you avoid facing an uncomfortable truth?

- What about your beliefs—do you consider their truth or question them? ■

ARE WE THERE YET?

There's a phrase I love in the Narcotics Anonymous literature that says their program isn't "a cure or a cure-all." We all want that cure, don't we? And authors always seem willing to promise that cure-all in the form of happiness, health, wealth, and enlightenment. For people like me who are drawn to such promises, there are quite a few years' worth of pursuing false leads and dead ends before we realize that there is no cure or cure-all.

When my daughter was younger, she had an all-purpose phrase to cover any disappointments: "Life is life." Our job then, it seems to me, is to get on with living as best we can. We can—and should—seek happiness, but that means we must engage and appreciate life as it's happening for us today, instead of believing we are moving toward some happy end. Ajahn Sumedho's famous evocation of this attitude is, "It's like this." "Pain in my knee is like this." "Sadness is like this." "Joy is like this."

I suppose that just brings us back once again to the simple genius of the Big Book: "Acceptance is the answer to my problems today . . ."

I'm no saint or genius, just a flawed human being with a certain gift for reflecting on and writing about some aspects of life—addiction, recovery, and Buddhism. I'm grateful that anyone thinks I'm worth listening to, and I sincerely hope that my words awaken something bright and alive in you, and in some small way, help you recover your joy.

May we all live in freedom and peace.

Kevin Griffin
December 17, 2014
Berkeley, California

WORKS CITED

Introduction

How We Choose to Be Happy: The 9 Choices of Extremely Happy People—Their Secrets, Their Stories, Rick Foster and Greg Hicks (Perigee Trade, 2004).

Chapter 1

Present Moment, Wonderful Moment: Mindfulness Verses for Daily Living, Thich Nhat Hanh (Parallax Press, 2006).

Chapter 2

Dharma Punx, Noah Levine (HarperOne, 2004).

Being Nobody, Going Nowhere: Meditations on the Buddhist Path, Ayya Khema (Wisdom Publications, 1987).

Christianity and Buddhism, Buddhadasa Bhikkhu (The Council of Thai Bhikkhus in U.S.A., 2007).

Alcoholics Anonymous (The Big Book), 4th ed. (Alcoholics Anonymous General Services, 2002).

The "Akron Pamphlets," Evan W. (Akron Area Intergroup Council of Alcoholics Anonymous).

Chapter 3

Lovingkindness: The Revolutionary Art of Happiness, Sharon Salzberg (Shambhala Publications, 2002).

Getting Love Right: Learning the Choices of Healthy Intimacy, Terence T. Gorski (Touchstone, 1993).

The Noble Eightfold Path: Way to the End of Suffering, Bhikkhu Bodhi (Pariyatti Publishing, 2006).

Chapter 5

The Heart of the Revolution: The Buddha's Radical Teachings on Forgiveness, Compassion, and Kindness, Noah Levine (HarperOne, 2011).

Right Concentration: A Practical Guide to the Jhanas, Leigh Brasington (Shambala Publications, available autumn 2015).

When the Iron Eagle Flies: Buddhism for the West, Ayya Khema (Wisdom Publications, 2000).

Chapter 6

Awakening Joy: 10 Steps to Happiness, James Baraz and Shoshana Alexander (Parallax Press, 2012).

Chapter 7

How to Be Sick: A Buddhist-Inspired Guide for the Chronically Ill and Their Caregivers, Toni Bernhard (Wisdom Publications, 2010).

Chi Kung in Recovery: Finding Your Way to a Balanced and Centered Recovery, Gregory Pergament (Central Recovery Press, 2013).

Mindful Eating: A Guide to Rediscovering a Healthy and Joyful Relationship with Food, Jan Chozen Bays (Shambhala Publications, 2009).

Chapter 8

The Mood Cure: The 4-Step Program to Take Charge of Your Emotions—Today, Julia Ross (Penguin Books, 2003).

Waking the Tiger: Healing Trauma, Peter A. Levine (North Atlantic Books, 1997).

Mindfulness-Based Cognitive Therapy for Depression, Zindel V. Segal, J. Mark G. Williams, and John D. Teasdale (The Guilford Press, 2012).

DBT Skills Training Manual, Marsha M. Linehan (The Guilford Press, 2014).

OTHER RECOMMENDED RESOURCES

Mindfulness

Mindfulness in Plain English, Bhante Gunaratana (Wisdom
Publications, 2011).

A Mindfulness-Based Stress Reduction Workbook, Bob Stahl and Elisha
Goldstein (New Harbinger Publications, 2010).

Wherever You Go, There You Are, Jon Kabat-Zinn (Hyperion, 2005).

Dharma

Breath by Breath: The Liberating Practice of Insight Meditation, Larry
Rosenberg (Shambhala Publications, 2004).

*Buddha's Nature: A Practical Guide to Discovering Your Place in the
Cosmos,* Wes Nisker (Bantam, 2000).

Buddhism without Beliefs: A Contemporary Guide to Awakening,
Stephen Batchelor (Riverhead Trade, 1998).

*The Experience of Insight: A Simple & Direct Guide to Buddhist
Meditation,* Joseph Goldstein (Shambhala Publications, 1987).

Mindfulness: A Practical Guide to Awakening, Joseph Goldstein
(Sounds True, 2013).

*A Path with Heart: A Guide through the Perils and Promises of Spiritual
Life,* Jack Kornfield (Bantam, 1993).

Who Is My Self? A Guide to Buddhist Meditation, Ayya Khema
(Wisdom Publications, 1997).

Sutta

In the Buddha's Words: An Anthology of Discourses from the Pali Canon,
edited by Bhikkhu Bodhi (Wisdom Publications, 2005).

*The Middle Length Discourses of the Buddha: A Translation of the
Majjhima Nikaya,* translated by Bhikkhu Nanamoli and Bhikkhu
Bodhi (Wisdom Publications, 1995).

Satipatthana: The Direct Path to Realization, Anālayo (Windhorse
Publications, 2004).

Buddhist Recovery

A Burning Desire: Dharma God & the Path of Recovery, Kevin Griffin
(Hay House, 2010).

Mindfulness and the 12 Steps: Living Recovery in the Present Moment,
Therese Jacobs-Stewart (Hazelden, 2010).

One Breath at a Time: Buddhism and the Twelve Steps, Kevin Griffin
(Rodale Books, 2004).

Twelve Steps

Basic Text of Narcotics Anonymous

Twelve Steps and Twelve Traditions

Other Useful Books

At Hell's Gate: A Soldier's Journey from War to Peace, Claude Anshin
Thomas (Shambhala Publications, 2013).

*The Mindful Way through Depression: Freeing Yourself from Chronic
Unhappiness,* Mark Williams, John Teasdale, Zindel Segal, and
John Kabat-Zinn (The Guilford Press, 2007).

Wide Awake: A Buddhist Guide for Teens, Diana Winston (Perigee
Trade, 2003).

Internet Resources

Access to Insight (accesstoinsight.org). Theravadan Buddhist site with
translations of and commentary on the Pali Canon.

Amaravati (amaravati.org). Website of Amaravati Monastery, the
main monastery for Western monks in the Thai Forest Tradition.

Awakening Joy (awakeningjoy.info). Website of James Baraz's great
workshop.

Buddhist Recovery Network (buddhistrecovery.org). Lists Buddhist
recovery meetings worldwide.

Dharma Seed (dharmaseed.org). Website for talks by vipassana and
Theravada teachers; many of my talks are available here.

Insight Meditation Society (dharma.org). Website for three centers
in Barre, Massachusetts: Insight Meditation Society (residential

group retreats), Barre Center for Buddhist Studies (residential study retreats), and Forest Refuge (residential self-retreats).

Kevin Griffin: Buddhism and Recovery (kevingriffin.net). My website. Find my teaching schedule here.

Leigh Brasington (leighb.com). Brasington is a dharma teacher who specializes in concentration practices. This site is a great resource for all kinds of topics related to Theravadan Buddhism.

Spirit Rock: An Insight Meditation Center (spiritrock.org). Website for Spirit Rock Meditation Center in Northern California. Teachings offered in residential retreats, daylong retreats, and evening classes.

ACKNOWLEDGMENTS

Writing these books doesn't get any easier for me, so I want to thank everyone who helped, guided, and motivated me along the way.

As with all my books, the inspiration comes from those I am supposed to inspire, the people who come to my classes, workshops, and retreats. I am grateful for their engagement and support. The centers where I teach and all their staff and volunteers do the really heavy lifting so I just have to show up. Spirit Rock Meditation Center, especially, has been a home for my teaching for many years.

I especially want to thank Sydney Faith Rose and Greg Pergament for their assistance teaching retreats.

And, in no particular order, thanks to all these friends and colleagues: Harry and Mora, Tom C., Heather Sundberg, Vimalasara, Walt Opie, Wes Nisker, George Johns, Don Lattin, Fran Didomenicis, Sean Fargo, Jay Stinnett, and Mary Stancavage.

My understanding of the dharma comes from the many teachers who I have been fortunate enough to meet, read, or listen to. You'll find many of their names in the resources section. James Baraz's work has had the most direct impact on my own work around happiness.

All the team at Sounds True have been incredibly helpful: Amy Rost's editing was smart, generous, and patient; Mitchell Clute made recording my CDs a breeze; and Jennifer Brown gave me confidence that this project would really work. Leslie Brown shepherded the project through production with patience and efficiency.

Stephanie Tade is a remarkable combination of agent, friend, and spiritual guide.

My wife, Rosemary Graham, and my daughter, Graham Griffin, remind me not to take myself too seriously, which might be the biggest key to happiness.

ABOUT THE AUTHOR

Kevin Griffin's first book, *One Breath at a Time* (Rodale, 2004), established him as a leader in the mindful recovery movement. Since its publication, Kevin has toured extensively, giving workshops and lectures throughout North America. He regularly teaches at leading dharma centers such as Spirit Rock Meditation Center and Southern Dharma Retreat Center, as well as at the Kripalu, Omega, and Esalen institutes. His writing and teaching have touched tens of thousands of recovering alcoholics, drug addicts, overeaters, and others who struggle with the wide range of addictions. He is a cofounder and board member of the Buddhist Recovery Network, an international organization that serves people in recovery. For more, please visit kevingriffin.net.

ABOUT SOUNDS TRUE

Sounds True is a multimedia publisher whose mission is to inspire and support personal transformation and spiritual awakening. Founded in 1985 and located in Boulder, Colorado, we work with many of the leading spiritual teachers, thinkers, healers, and visionary artists of our time. We strive with every title to preserve the essential "living wisdom" of the author or artist. It is our goal to create products that not only provide information to a reader or listener, but that also embody the quality of a wisdom transmission.

For those seeking genuine transformation, Sounds True is your trusted partner. At SoundsTrue.com you will find a wealth of free resources to support your journey, including exclusive weekly audio interviews, free downloads, interactive learning tools, and other special savings on all our titles.

To learn more, please visit SoundsTrue.com/freegifts or call us toll-free at 800-333-9185.

SOUNDS TRUE
many voices, one journey